Better Homes and Gardens.

MORE FROM YOUR WOK

CREDITS

On the cover:
Festive Chicken (see recipe, page 33)
Broccoli and Fish Bundles (see recipe, page 37)
Toasted Coconut Custard (see recipe, page 79)

BETTER HOMES AND GARDENS® BOOKS
Editor: Gerald M. Knox
Art Director: Ernest Shelton
Managing Editor: David A. Kirchner

Food and Nutrition Editor: Doris Eby
Department Head Cook Books: Sharyl Heiken
Senior Food Editor: Elizabeth Woolever
Senior Associate Food Editors: Sandra Granseth, Rosemary C. Hutchinson
Associate Food Editors: Jill Burmeister, Julia Martinusen, Diana McMillen,
    Marcia Stanley, Diane Yanney
Recipe Development Editor: Marion Viall
Test Kitchen Director: Sharon Stilwell
Test Kitchen Home Economists: Jean Brekke, Kay Cargill, Marilyn Cornelius,
    Maryellyn Krantz, Marge Steenson

Associate Art Director (Managing): Randall Yontz
Associate Art Directors (Creative): Linda Ford, Neoma Alt West
Copy and Production Editors: Nancy Nowiszewski,
    Lamont Olson, Mary Helen Schiltz, David A. Walsh
Assistant Art Directors: Faith Berven, Harijs Priekulis
Graphic Designers: Mike Burns, Alisann Dixon, Mike Eagleton, Lynda
    Haupert, Deb Miner, Lyne Neymeyer, Bill Shaw, D. Greg Thompson

Editor in Chief: Neil Kuehnl
Group Editorial Services Director: Duane L. Gregg
Executive Art Director: William J. Yates

General Manager: Fred Stines
Director of Publishing: Robert B. Nelson
Director of Retail Marketing: Jamie Martin
Director of Direct Marketing: Arthur Heydendael

MORE FROM YOUR WOK
Editors: Sharyl Heiken, Elizabeth Woolever
Copy and Production Editor: David A. Walsh
Graphic Designer: Lynda Haupert
Consultant: Flora Szatkowski

Our seal assures you that every recipe in *More From Your Wok* is endorsed by the Better Homes and Gardens Test Kitchen. Each recipe is tested for family appeal, practicality, and deliciousness.

CONTENTS

UNDERSTANDING THE WOK

If you think a wok is just a pan for preparing Oriental food, think again. Sure, you can cook terrific Oriental meals in your wok, but it's also great for American stews, Mexican tamales, and Italian spaghetti. And, there is nothing difficult about wok cooking. This first chapter will help you choose the right wok and accessories to go with it, use the tools to best advantage, and learn the basic wok-cooking techniques: stir-frying, simmering, deep-fat frying, and steaming. Soon you will be using your wok every day!

electric wok

perforated steamer rack

bamboo brush

wire strainer

steel wok

stacking aluminum
steamer racks

bamboo steamer rack
with lid

stainless steel wok with
deep-fat frying rack

ring stand

deep-fat frying
thermometer

chopsticks

cleaver

spatula

UNDERSTANDING THE WOK

Choosing a Wok

The wok is one of the most versatile pans you'll ever own. Its sloping sides make it a superior shape for stir-frying, deep-fat frying, simmering, and steaming nearly any kind of food.

But all woks are not the same; they vary in size, shape, material, and accessories. With so many to choose from, consider the features you need for your purposes.

A 14- to 16-inch-diameter wok is perfect for a household range, and it's the most-common size in most stores. Expect to stir-fry 2 to 4 servings of a main dish in this size. Much larger woks are available, but unless you have special cooking facilities, they are difficult to use at home. If you need greater capacity, purchase two woks and enlist someone to help you with the cooking.

The most common material used in making woks is a carbon or tempered steel. This type of steel requires thorough initial seasoning, and additional care each time it is used. It will quickly acquire a dark, well-used appearance. Its good heat-transfer characteristics make it an excellent wok for stir-frying and deep-fat frying. However, if you plan to simmer and steam often, choose another type of material; prolonged moist heat can cause rust formation that will discolor this type of wok and food prepared in it.

Stainless steel is now used for many woks. It does not discolor or rust, but it transfers heat less quickly than does carbon steel. To amend this characteristic, some manufacturers wrap the exterior heating surface with aluminum or copper. Stainless steel woks are very attractive and require less care than do carbon steel woks.

Woks made of aluminum and aluminum alloys are increasing in popularity. They have good heating properties and need little care. Some tend to darken with use, but a good aluminum cleaner can remedy that. One alloy is black when new, and avoids that problem.

Check to see what material makes up the wok's lid, too. If yours is carbon steel, it needs to be rubbed occasionally with oil to prevent rust. Some steel woks are equipped with aluminum lids that do not rust.

The shape of the lid is important when using the wok as a steamer. A high dome lid will accommodate larger pieces of meat or baking dishes than a flat lid will.

Most woks perform efficiently on a gas range. If you have an electric range, choose a wok that will allow you to place it very close to the burner. Electric heat works best when it makes contact with the pan, so look for a flat-bottomed wok with a ring stand that supports the wok directly on the unit or a flat-bottomed design that doesn't require a ring stand at all. If you can't find one, settle for a wok that fits very close to the unit. See page 8 for proper placement of the stand.

Another feature to consider is the handle or handles. Steel or aluminum handles quickly become hot during cooking, so you must remember to use potholders with them. Some woks have wooden handles that insulate the metal parts. Other woks have a long handle that is convenient for holding the wok steady during stir-frying. An additional handle on the opposite side facilitates carrying the wok when it is full.

Electric Woks

An electric wok gives wok cooking portable possibilities. You can stir-fry or deep-fat fry at the dinner table with friends joining in. Or let the wok double as a food warmer on a buffet line.

Early electric woks were unable to reach the high temperatures required for satisfactory stir-frying, but today's models have improved. The only significant difference in operation between an electric and a conventional wok is that the electric wok's thermostat causes the heat to cycle on and off. You may notice a change in the speed of boiling at times, but the cycling should not affect the finished product. And, the thermostatic control makes successful deep-fat frying easy.

Many electric woks are made of brightly painted aluminum and lined with a non-stick coating for easy cleaning. Others are stainless steel inside and out, or stainless steel clad with copper or aluminum. Electric woks generally have a removable heat-control unit, so the wok can be immersed for cleaning.

When you purchase an electric wok, be sure to read the manufacturer's directions for using it and for seasoning its interior.

Accessories

Just as there are many different kinds of woks, there are a multitude of accessories. Fortunately, a wok needs few accessories. Aside from a ring stand, the only other essential for stir-frying is a long-handled spatula or spoon; for deep-fat frying you need a wire strainer or slotted spoon and a deep-fat frying thermometer; and for steaming, some type of rack is necessary.

Other accessories may be fun to use, or decorative, or handy. Refer to the photograph on pages 4 and 5 for an idea of how they look, keeping in mind the many variations you may find at your store. The brief descriptions below will help you use them to best advantage, and suggest alternatives.

● **Ring stand:** Most important to the stability of the wok is its stand. Although some stands have straight sides, most are tapered so you can adjust the wok's distance from the heat (see page 8 for the proper way to use a tapered ring stand). Some woks with large, flat bottoms do not require stands, but sit directly on the unit.

● **Steamer rack:** Steamer racks are made from many different materials and come in many sizes and styles, but their function is the same. They hold food over simmering water, allowing steam to surround the food and cook it. Some steamer racks can be stacked to cook several foods at the same time, saving energy and keeping the kitchen cool. These racks, made of aluminum or bamboo, have their own snug lids.

Other steamer racks are simply flat rounds of perforated metal that settle partway down the wok's sides. Some steamer racks are flat, wire mesh rounds; others are perforated metal plates with expanding petals that fit in any sort of pan. Not to be overlooked are woven bamboo racks that resemble trivets, and collapsible racks made of bamboo sticks.

When choosing a steamer rack, consider the quantity and type of food you'll want to cook. Don't pay extra for several tiers if you'll only use one at a time. Make sure the spaces are too small for foods to slip through when you steam without a dish. See page 13 for ways to improvise a steamer rack for your wok.

● **Deep-fat frying rack:** This semicircular or doughnut-shaped wire rack hangs from the sides of the wok. Use it when you deep-fat fry to drain the food and keep it warm. The advantage of the rack is that the oil drains off the food back into the wok, instead of onto paper toweling; but a rack is not essential to deep-fat frying in a wok.

● **Cleaver:** Used for every chopping and cutting task you can imagine, a cleaver is an easy-to-handle, wide-bladed knife. It is especially handy for all the slicing, chopping, and mincing required in stir-frying. To use it properly, grasp the cleaver blade between the thumb and index finger; wrap the remaining 3 fingers around the handle in a firm hold. Use your other hand to guide the food, curling your fingertips under, and holding your knuckles against the flat side of the cleaver blade (see the illustration on page 9). If you don't have a cleaver, any good knife will do.

● **Spatula:** Indispensable in stir-frying is a long-handled utensil for keeping food in motion over the high heat. A Chinese-style spatula has a wide, slightly curved, metal blade that is perfect for the job; a long-handled spoon or wooden spoon is a good second choice. For non-stick surfaces, choose wood or another material that will not damage the finish.

● **Wire strainer:** When deep-fat frying, a wire strainer is perfect for adding food to the hot oil, then removing it when done. A fine wire mesh discourages the oil from clinging, and a wooden handle protects your hand from the intense heat. Use a slotted spoon for this task, if you prefer.

● **Deep-fat frying thermometer:** The temperature of the fat is the single most important factor in successful deep-fat frying, and a thermometer helps you monitor it. However, not all deep-fat frying thermometers are suited to a wok. Choose one long enough to clip on the side of the wok, but made so the bulb does not contact the wok. Before buying one, check the fit in a wok to make sure it meets these criteria. If you don't mind holding the thermometer in the fat, you can use any deep-fat frying thermometer.

● **Bamboo brush:** Just the thing for scrubbing your wok, a bamboo brush is a gentle Oriental scouring pad. If you don't have one, use a sponge or nylon or plastic scrubber to clean your wok. Don't use abrasive implements, which could damage non-stick or seasoned surfaces.

● **Other accessories:** Your wok also may be equipped with a long-handled ladle for serving, and chopsticks for mixing, cooking, and eating your wok creations.

UNDERSTANDING THE WOK

Caring for Your Wok

Like any cooking tool, your wok needs care to perform well. Just a few minutes of attention each time you use it will preserve it for many years of good cooking.

A new carbon-steel wok comes with a coating of rust-resistant material that has been applied by the manufacturer. You must remove this coating before you can use the wok. To do so, scrub the wok thoroughly inside and out with cleanser or scouring pads and hot, soapy water. Rinse the wok carefully, then dry it with a towel. To be sure the wok is completely dry, heat it on your range for a few minutes.

The initial seasoning is most important for the optimum performance of a steel wok. Add 2 tablespoons cooking oil to the wok; heat the oil over high heat till the wok and oil are very hot. Tilt and rotate the wok until the oil coats the entire inner surface. Allow the wok to cool, then dry it, rubbing thoroughly with paper toweling.

If the wok comes with a steel lid, you should also scrub and coat it with oil when you season the wok. Otherwise, moisture that condenses on the lid during cooking can cause it to rust.

Each time you use the steel wok, you must clean and reseason it. Soak the wok in hot water (detergent is unnecessary), then clean it well with a bamboo brush or sponge. Rinse thoroughly, then dry with a towel. Heat the wok on the range to ensure it is totally dry. Add about a teaspoon of cooking oil to the wok and rub it in with paper toweling. Thoroughly clean and dry the wok's lid and rub with oil (if the lid is steel).

Resist the temptation to put your wok in the dishwasher; the harsh detergents and hot water will destroy the seasoning you've worked so hard to obtain.

Store your wok in a well-ventilated place, perhaps hanging on a wall or displayed on a counter. Long periods in a warm, airless cupboard can cause the oil used in seasoning the wok to become rancid.

Aluminum and stainless steel woks require no seasoning, but still need certain care. Keep these woks clean, using a stainless steel or aluminum cleaner, if necessary.

Woks with an interior non-stick coating need seasoning, too, but the method depends on the type of coating each has. Follow the manufacturer's directions for your wok. Most non-stick coatings need a thorough cleaning and drying, then a small amount of cooking oil rubbed over the interior surface. As with steel woks, they need open storage. And they must never be scrubbed with an abrasive surface; instead use one of the plastic scrubbing pads specifically designed for non-stick coatings.

Electric woks deserve special consideration. Follow the care directions recommended for the interior surface material in your wok.

If your wok is immersible for washing, be sure to remove any parts not immersible, such as the heat control. Thoroughly dry every part of the wok before you reassemble it or plug it in. Be sure to read and follow the use and care guide prepared by the manufacturer of your electric wok.

Using a Ring Stand

Electric Range: If your wok has a tapered ring stand, turn the wide side up for use on your electric range. This allows the wok to sit closer to the electric heating unit for more-efficient cooking.

Gas Range: Place the ring stand with its narrow side up over your largest gas burner for best results on a gas range. The elevation of the wok actually places it over a hotter part of the gas flame for better heating.

Cutting Terms

Slice

Make even cuts with a knife or cleaver into the meat or vegetable, perpendicular to the cutting board. Most often slices should be ⅛ to ¼ inch thick. When a recipe calls for thin slices, make cuts as close together as possible. Slicing provides an even cross section in pieces and is used in all cooking methods.

Roll-cut

Hold knife or cleaver at an angle to make first cut, then give food a quarter- to half-turn before angle-cutting again. This cut is used for cylindrical vegetables to produce unusual shapes. Generally roll-cut slices need more cooking time than simple slices, and these pieces sometimes need blanching before stir-frying.

Bias-slice

Hold the knife or cleaver at an angle while you cut the food into slices. The pieces cut this way have a greater surface area, so they will cook more quickly. That's why this cut is often used for firmer vegetables used in stir-frying. The additional surface area not only speeds cooking, but also adds visual appeal.

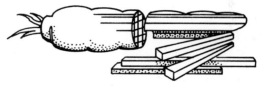

Julienne

Cut the food into long, narrow strips resembling matchsticks. First, cut the food into slices about 2 inches long and ¼ to ½ inch thick. Stack the slices, then slice lengthwise again to make these thin sticks. Besides their attractiveness, julienne strips cook very quickly because of their large surface area.

Slicing Meat

Stir-frying does a wonderful job of cooking most cuts of meat. Part of the secret of stir-frying is in the way the meat is cut before cooking begins. Slice it very thinly across the grain for optimum tenderness. The easy way to do this is to freeze the meat until it is firm, but not hard, before slicing. Allow 45 to 60 minutes in the freezer to make the meat firm enough to slice. Then use a very sharp knife or cleaver to cut across the meat's grain into slices as thin as possible. If the meat slices are large, cut them into bite-size pieces.

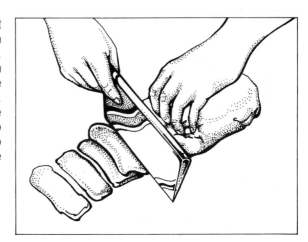

COOKING METHODS

Stir-Fry

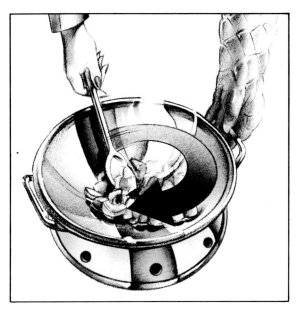 

Woks are specially designed for stir-frying, a cooking technique in which foods are cooked quickly in a little oil. The key to the fast cooking is the way food is prepared. First it is cut or chopped into very thin or small pieces, then fried over very high heat. This procedure is extremely effective in preserving the flavor, nutrition, and color of foods.

Stir-frying is traditionally regarded as an Oriental cooking technique, but you'll find it's practically the same as the French sauté. And you'll be pleasantly surprised to see what stir-frying can do for Italian pasta, Indian curry, and your other favorite foods.

Because the food cooks so quickly, you must have all ingredients ready before you begin cooking. The first step in stir-frying then, is to cut up the meat, vegetables, and other ingredients you plan to use. Some vegetables may need blanching in boiling water before you can stir-fry them. And sometimes a recipe will call for cooked rice or pasta; start cooking them so they'll be ready when you need them.

Arrange all the ingredients on dishes near the wok, so you can reach them easily when you are ready for them.

Many Oriental stir-fried dishes are seasoned and thickened with a soy sauce-cornstarch mixture added to the wok toward the end of the cooking process. (In other cuisines, this mixture may be flour mixed with broth, milk, or wine.) Combine these ingredients before beginning to stir-fry, then stir them again just before adding to the wok.

When everything is ready, place the wok over a burner set on high heat. When the wok is hot, add the cooking oil in a ring around the upper part of the wok so it coats the sides as it runs to the center of the wok. When the oil is hot, proceed with cooking the vegetables and meats as directed in the recipe.

Usually, pungent seasonings such as garlic and gingerroot are cooked first. Then slower-cooking vegetables are stir-fried, followed by those that cook more quickly. Meat, chicken, or fish is generally the last item to be stir-fried.

Never overload the wok with food, or the cooking speed will be slowed. Instead, divide large amounts of food and cook only part at a time. When you remove food from the wok, add more oil, if needed, for the next batch of food, and bring it up to cooking temperature before proceeding.

Use a spatula or a long-handled spoon for stir-frying the food. Gently lift and turn the food with a folding motion so it cooks evenly. It's important to keep the food moving at all times; otherwise it will quickly burn on the very high heat.

To add the thickening mixture, push the cooked food up the sides of the wok, leaving the center clear of food. Stir the liquid mixture and add it to the center of the wok, as shown above. Cook and stir till the mixture is thickened and bubbly; cook and stir 1 or 2 minutes longer to ensure that the thickening agent is completely cooked. Now stir all the ingredients together and heat through. Serve at once to preserve the fresh color and flavor of the foods.

For best results when stir-frying with cooking oil, always use high heat. However, when you use butter, margarine, or another fat, use a slightly lower temperature; these fats tend to burn when cooked over high heat.

Most woks are large enough to stir-fry up to 4 servings of a main dish. Don't try to prepare more, or the quality will suffer. Instead, take out a second wok and have a helper cook alongside you. Use either the same recipe or another one for variety. The work can be twice as much fun, and the results twice as delicious.

Simmer

No doubt simmering is an often-used technique in your household for making stews, pot roasts, and one-dish meals. Now you'll discover how well a wok does the task, for everything from appetizer sausages to pilaf to fruit desserts.

The transition from stir-frying to simmering (or braising) is a natural one for the wok. Most simmered foods begin with a stir-frying step. This stir-frying starts the recipe off right by precooking some foods and distributing the flavors of seasonings such as garlic and onions. Browning the meat before simmering adds color and flavor to the finished dish.

A liquid is added, and the simmering process takes over to tenderize larger pieces or tougher cuts of meat, to fully cook starchy foods such as rice and potatoes, and to mellow the flavors of the foods over a longer period of time.

To begin the simmering process, the meat is usually browned in cooking oil or another fat. Onions and other flavorful vegetables are often stir-fried in a little fat until they are tender. Drain off all excess fat to avoid a greasy finished product.

Now add liquid and bring the mixture in the wok to boiling. Reduce the heat so the food simmers (that is, a few small bubbles will form slowly and burst before reaching the surface of the liquid).

If a gravy is desired, add a mixture of flour or cornstarch and liquid to the wok when the food is done; cook and stir constantly until the mixture is thickened and bubbly. Cook and stir 1 or 2 minutes longer in order to cook the starch thoroughly. Serve at once.

For long cooking, cover the wok to keep the liquid inside the wok and the steam out of the kitchen. Leave the wok uncovered if you want to reduce the mixture's quantity or thicken it slightly.

Be sure your steel wok and its lid are well-seasoned before using them for simmering. Otherwise you may experience discoloration of both the wok itself and the food in it. Some foods such as beer and red wine are particularly apt to cause this kind of discoloration. Although the change in appearance doesn't necessarily affect the taste or safety of the food, it is visually unappetizing.

COOKING METHODS

Deep-Fat Fry

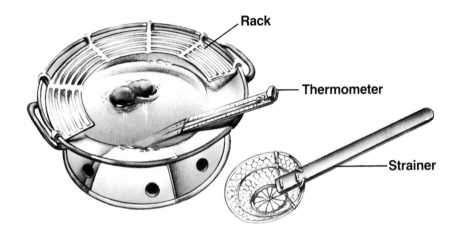

Rack

Thermometer

Strainer

Although it doesn't look like a deep-fat fryer, a wok doubles as one easily. And, because of its unique shape, it generally requires less cooking oil to do so.

Safety, always important in the kitchen, becomes paramount when you have very hot oil in a potentially unstable pan. Be sure your wok is very solidly placed in its ring stand on the burner before you add the oil.

Use 1 to 1½ inches cooking oil for most foods; you may need 2 inches of oil for larger pieces of food. Measure the depth of the oil at its deepest point in the center of the wok. Generally you'll be using 3 to 4 cups of cooking oil.

Choose an oil that can be heated to a very high temperature without smoking. Peanut oil is very popular in Oriental kitchens, but corn, cottonseed, and other vegetable oils are also suitable.

Heat the oil to the temperature indicated in the recipe, usually 365° to 375°. Use a long, flat thermometer like the one pictured on pages 4 and 5, or any deep-fat frying thermometer that will rest in the wok with its bulb in the oil, but not touching the pan itself.

Maintaining a constant temperature is very important. Too low a temperature will produce greasy food; too high a temperature will cause the center to be underdone and the exterior to burn. Using the proper temperature produces food that is moist inside and golden outside.

Be careful when adding food to the oil. The moisture in the food can make the oil spatter, and cause serious burns. Add the food to the wok by lowering it into the fat with a wire strainer or a slotted spoon.

Keep quantities small enough to avoid lowering the oil's temperature too much. And be sure to allow the oil to recover its proper temperature before adding more food.

Remove the food from the wok with a wire strainer or slotted spoon. Try to remove all bits of food that may have broken off during frying before they have a chance to burn.

Drain the fried food on a wire rack or on several layers of paper toweling. Some woks come with a semicircular or round wire rack that fits over the edge of the wok to drain the food and keep it hot (see photo, pages 4 and 5).

If you're preparing a large amount of food, spread the deep-fat fried food in one layer on a baking sheet lined with paper toweling. Keep it warm in a 250° oven until serving time.

After frying, allow the oil to cool in the wok before trying to remove it. Strain the cooled oil through a double thickness of cheesecloth into jars or other storage containers. Cover tightly and store in the refrigerator. Before reusing the oil, add an equal amount of new oil to freshen the old, and to prevent smoking and flare-ups.

You can deep-fat fry at the dinner table if you have an electric wok or a very stable, heavy electric hot plate for your conventional wok. Set the wok on a heat-proof tray to protect the table from spattering oil, spills, and heat from the unit. Heat the oil right at the table so you don't have to carry the hot oil. Provide diners with long-handled forks or individual strainers so they can cook their own food. Tempura (see recipe, page 42) and Crunchy Meatball Fondue (see recipe, page 85) are good choices for frying at the table.

Steam

Rack

The wok's sloping sides make it ideal for steaming foods, too. Just add a steamer rack and boiling water, and you're ready to create spectacular dishes you never thought could come from a wok: one-burner meals, fresh-tasting vegetables, and luscious steamed puddings and cakes.

Many woks have steamer racks. Some racks are perforated metal rounds; others are fashioned of bamboo. Some Oriental cooks simply cross chopsticks in the wok for a homemade rack.

Multi-layered bamboo steamer racks are designed expressly for use with the wok, and let you cook several different dishes at once. Stackable aluminum steamer racks also are available and are perfectly suited for use with a wok.

But you may already have a workable steamer rack in your kitchen. A round wire cooling rack or a small metal colander would work quite well. Or punch holes in a disposable foil pie pan and invert it in the wok to make an excellent substitute.

Your steel wok must be well-seasoned when used for steaming. Be sure to have both the wok and the lid well coated with cooking oil, then dried. If not, rust may form on both during the steaming process.

Steaming is an easy cooking method. First, pour boiling water into the wok to reach about ½ inch below the steamer rack. Now arrange the food directly on the steamer rack (or place dish of food on the rack). Cover the wok and cook over simmering water until the food is done. The steam sends an even heat circulating throughout the wok, cooking food quickly. And there's never any danger of burning the food.

When a recipe requires a dish in addition to the steamer rack, choose one that is heatproof and fits on the steamer rack without covering all the openings. This allows the steam to freely circulate around the dish. Metal pans are suitable, as are heatproof glass and ceramic dishes.

Often, the food in dishes is covered with foil so the steam will not condense into the food and make it soggy. This is especially important for puddings, custards, and breads that could be ruined by the additional water.

Make sure the wok's lid closes the wok tightly so steam loss is minimal. If a dish or piece of food is too large for the wok's lid to fit snugly, improvise a larger lid from foil. Use two pieces of heavy foil joined side by side, or crisscross them across the top of the wok; crimp tightly to the sides of the wok to preserve the steam.

When you're steaming for a long time, check the water under the steamer rack occasionally to make sure it hasn't boiled dry. Add more water, if necessary; use boiling water to keep the temperature high. (Don't peek too often or you will lose valuable cooking steam from the wok, and the dish will require additional time.)

Any time you remove the lid from a steaming wok, do so carefully. The built-up steam can burn you immediately.

To cook more than one dish at a time in your steamer, see the tip on page 39.

Veal in Cream Sauce
(see recipe, page 21)

Fiesta Tostadas (see
recipe, page 25)

Pictured below: Paella
(see recipe, page 42)

In addition to an appetizing collection of meat, poultry, and seafood entrées, you can prepare exciting meatless main dishes in your wok. To help solve the problem of leftovers, this chapter includes 16 inventive ways to use them; choose a recipe and add whatever is left over at your house.

BEEF, PORK, and LAMB

Hungarian Goulash

1¼ **pounds beef top round steak**
¼ **cup butter** *or* **margarine**
2 **large onions, chopped**
1 **green pepper, chopped**
1 **7½-ounce can tomatoes, cut up**
¾ **cup beef broth**
3 **tablespoons paprika**
¾ **cup dairy sour cream**
3 **tablespoons all-purpose flour**
   Hot cooked noodles

Partially freeze beef; thinly slice across grain into bite-size strips. In wok melt butter over medium-high heat. Add *half* the beef and stir-fry till browned; remove. Repeat with remaining beef. Stir-fry onions and green pepper till tender. Return beef to wok. Stir in *undrained* tomatoes, broth, paprika, and 1 teaspoon *salt*. Cover and simmer 10 to 15 minutes or till meat is tender. Blend together sour cream and flour; gradually stir in about *1 cup* hot mixture. Return all to wok. Cook and stir till thickened and bubbly; cook and stir 1 minute longer. Serve over noodles. Makes 6 servings.

Burgundy Beef

1 **pound beef flank steak** *or* **beef top round steak**
1 **medium green pepper**
¾ **cup beef broth**
½ **cup white burgundy***
3 **tablespoons all-purpose flour**
½ **teaspoon salt**
⅛ **teaspoon pepper**
2 **tablespoons cooking oil**
1½ **cups sliced fresh mushrooms**
1½ **cups frozen small whole onions**
   Hot cooked noodles

Partially freeze beef; thinly slice across grain into bite-size strips. Cut green pepper into 1-inch squares. Mix broth, wine, flour, salt, and pepper; set aside. Heat wok over high heat; add oil. Stir-fry *half* of meat 2 to 3 minutes or till just brown; remove. Repeat with remaining meat. Stir-fry mushrooms and onions over medium-high heat 4 minutes or till almost tender. Add green pepper; stir-fry 5 minutes. Stir wine mixture; add to wok. Cook and stir till thickened and bubbly; cook and stir 1 minute longer. Return beef to wok; heat through. Serve over hot noodles. Makes 6 servings.

  *Recipe note: Red wine tends to discolor in a steel wok, but if yours has a non-stick coating, you may prefer to use red burgundy in this recipe.

Ribs with Horseradish Sauce

2 **tablespoons cooking oil**
4 **pounds beef short ribs**
2 **medium onions, sliced**
2 **medium carrots, sliced**
2 **stalks celery, cut into 1-inch pieces**
1 **cup tomato juice**
½ **teaspoon salt**
⅛ **teaspoon pepper**
2 **tablespoons all-purpose flour**
1 **tablespoon prepared horseradish**

Heat wok over high heat; add oil. Brown ribs, a few at a time, in hot oil. Drain off fat. Return all ribs to wok; add onions, carrots, celery, tomato juice, salt, and pepper. Bring to boiling; reduce heat. Cover and simmer about 2 hours or till ribs are tender. Remove ribs and vegetables to platter; keep warm.

   Skim fat from cooking liquid. Pour off cooking liquid, reserving 1½ cups; return reserved liquid to wok. Combine flour and ¼ cup cold *water;* stir into cooking liquid in wok. Stir in horseradish. Cook and stir till thickened and bubbly; cook and stir 1 minute longer. Spoon sauce over ribs on platter. Makes 4 to 6 servings.

Beer-Sauced Meatballs

1 beaten egg
¾ cup soft bread crumbs
2 tablespoons catsup
1 teaspoon Worcestershire
   sauce
½ teaspoon chili powder
1 pound ground beef
1 tablespoon cooking oil
2 medium onions, sliced
2 tablespoons all-purpose flour
1 cup beer
   Hot cooked noodles

In bowl combine egg, bread crumbs, catsup, Worcestershire sauce, chili powder, and ½ teaspoon *salt*. Add meat; mix well. Shape into 1-inch meatballs.

Heat wok over medium-high heat; add oil. Cook *half* the meatballs at a time, shaking wok to brown on all sides. Remove all meatballs from wok. Reserve 2 tablespoons drippings in wok. Add onions to wok; stir-fry over medium-high heat about 6 minutes or till tender. Stir in flour, ½ teaspoon *salt,* and ⅛ teaspoon *pepper.* Stir in beer. Cook and stir till thickened and bubbly. Return meatballs to wok; cover and simmer 10 minutes. Serve over hot cooked noodles. Makes 4 or 5 servings.

No-Chop Stir-Fry

3 tablespoons soy sauce
1 tablespoon cornstarch
½ cup water
3 tablespoons dry sherry
1 teaspoon instant beef bouillon
   granules
½ teaspoon ground ginger
1 pound ground beef*
1 tablespoon cooking oil
1 8-ounce can sliced water
   chestnuts, drained
1 cup fresh bean sprouts
1 6-ounce package frozen pea
   pods, thawed
½ cup peanuts

Stir soy sauce into cornstarch; stir in water, sherry, bouillon granules, and ginger. Set aside. Shape beef into ¾-inch meatballs. Heat wok over high heat; add oil. Stir-fry meatballs for 3 minutes or till browned. Drain off excess fat. Add water chestnuts, bean sprouts, and pea pods. Stir-fry 1 minute. Stir soy mixture; add to wok. Cook and stir till thickened and bubbly; cook and stir 2 minutes longer. Stir in peanuts. Serve over chow mein noodles or hot cooked rice, if desired. Makes 4 to 6 servings.

*Recipe note: Vary this recipe by substituting ground pork or ground lamb for the beef.

Beefy Spanish Rice

3 slices bacon, cut up
1 medium onion, chopped
1 small green pepper, chopped
1 pound ground beef
1 cup long grain rice
1 16-ounce can tomatoes, cut up
1 4-ounce can taco sauce
1 teaspoon Worcestershire
   sauce
1 cup shredded cheddar cheese

In wok cook bacon over medium-high heat till crisp; drain, reserving drippings in wok. Set bacon aside. Stir-fry onion and green pepper in drippings 3 to 5 minutes; remove. Cook beef in wok, stirring often, till brown. Drain off fat. Return onion and pepper to wok. Add uncooked rice; stir-fry 2 minutes. Stir in *undrained* tomatoes, taco sauce, Worcestershire, 2 cups *water,* ½ teaspoon *salt,* and ⅛ teaspoon *pepper.* Bring to boiling. Reduce heat; cover and simmer 15 to 20 minutes or till liquid is absorbed and rice is done. Top with cheese and bacon; cover and cook 1 minute. Makes 4 to 6 servings.

BEEF, PORK, and LAMB

Mexican Stuffed Peppers

6 medium red *or* green peppers
1 beaten egg
1 8-ounce can tomato sauce
1 cup cooked rice
½ cup raisins
1 teaspoon chili powder
½ teaspoon salt
¼ teaspoon ground cinnamon
⅛ teaspoon ground cloves
1 pound lean ground beef
¾ cup shredded Monterey Jack
    cheese (3 ounces)

Slice tops off red or green peppers. Finely chop the tops, discarding membranes and seeds. In bowl combine chopped peppers and egg; stir in tomato sauce, rice, raisins, chili powder, salt, cinnamon, and cloves. Add ground beef; mix well. Spoon mixture evenly into peppers.

Pour boiling water into wok to reach ½ inch below steamer rack. Arrange peppers upright on steamer rack. Cover wok and steam for 50 to 60 minutes or till meat is done and peppers are tender. Top with cheese. Makes 6 servings.

Beef and Pepper Spaghetti

6 beef cubed steaks
1 large green pepper
2 tablespoons cooking oil
1 cup sliced fresh mushrooms
½ teaspoon dried basil, crushed
1 clove garlic, minced
1 16-ounce jar spaghetti sauce
    Hot cooked spaghetti
¾ cup shredded mozzarella
    cheese (3 ounces)

Cut beef and green pepper into ½-inch-wide strips. Heat wok over high heat; add cooking oil. Stir-fry the meat, *half* at a time, till browned; remove meat from wok. Stir-fry green pepper, mushrooms, basil, and garlic for 3 to 5 minutes or till vegetables are tender. Stir in spaghetti sauce and meat. Reduce heat; cover and simmer for 10 to 15 minutes, stirring often. Serve over hot cooked spaghetti; sprinkle with cheese. Makes 6 servings.

Continental Beef Stew

1½ pounds beef stew meat
2 ears fresh corn on the cob
3 tablespoons cooking oil
1 medium onion, chopped
1 clove garlic, minced
1 16-ounce can tomatoes, cut up
½ cup dry red wine
2 tablespoons snipped parsley
1 teaspoon sugar
1 teaspoon salt
½ teaspoon dried thyme,
    crushed
¼ teaspoon pepper
¼ cup all-purpose flour
    Hot cooked rice

Cut beef into 1-inch cubes; cut corn into 1-inch pieces. Heat wok over medium-high heat. Add oil. Stir-fry meat, *half* at a time, in the hot oil till browned. Remove meat from wok. Stir-fry onion and garlic till onion is tender. Drain off excess fat. Return meat to wok. Stir in *undrained* tomatoes, wine, parsley, sugar, salt, thyme, pepper, and ¾ cup *water.* Bring to boiling; reduce heat. Cover and simmer 40 minutes. Add corn; cover and simmer about 20 minutes longer or till meat is tender. Combine flour and ⅓ cup cold *water;* stir into meat mixture. Cook and stir till thickened and bubbly; cook and stir 1 minute longer. Serve over hot rice. Makes 6 servings.

BEEF, PORK, and LAMB

Corned Beef Platter

1 3- to 4-pound corned beef brisket
4 large sweet potatoes, peeled and cut into 1-inch pieces (4 cups)
6 to 8 small boiling onions
2 tablespoons brown sugar
1 tablespoon cornstarch
1 20-ounce can pineapple chunks
Snipped parsley

Pour boiling water into wok to reach ½ inch below steamer rack. Place corned beef on rack; pour any juices and spices from package into wok. Cover wok and steam for 2 hours, adding water to wok as needed. Add potatoes and onions to steamer rack; cover wok and steam 25 minutes or till meat and vegetables are done.

In saucepan stir together sugar and cornstarch. Slowly stir in small amount of syrup from pineapple. Stir in remaining syrup and pineapple. Cook and stir till thickened and bubbly; cook and stir 2 minutes more. Arrange meat and vegetables on platter; spoon pineapple mixture over. Top with parsley. Makes 6 to 8 servings.

Sherried Liver with Mushrooms

1 pound calf liver
3 tablespoons dry sherry
1 tablespoon cornstarch
¼ cup chicken broth
½ teaspoon sugar
½ teaspoon dried basil, crushed
¼ teaspoon salt
2 tablespoons cooking oil
1 clove garlic, minced
1 large green pepper, cut into strips
1 small onion, sliced
2 cups sliced fresh mushrooms
6 cherry tomatoes, halved

Cut liver into narrow strips. Sprinkle liver strips with sherry; let stand at room temperature 30 minutes, stirring occasionally. Drain liver, reserving sherry. Stir cornstarch into reserved sherry; stir in broth, sugar, basil, and salt. Set aside.

Heat wok over high heat; add oil. Stir-fry garlic in hot oil 30 seconds. Add green pepper and onion; stir-fry 1 to 2 minutes. Remove vegetables. Add mushrooms to wok; stir-fry 1 minute. Remove from wok.

Add more oil to wok if needed. Add liver to hot oil in wok; stir-fry 2 minutes. Stir broth mixture; stir into liver. Cook and stir till thickened and bubbly; cook and stir 2 minutes more. Return vegetables to wok. Arrange tomatoes atop. Cover and cook 2 minutes. Serve immediately with hot cooked noodles, if desired. Makes 4 servings.

Take Your Wok to a Barbecue

When it's too hot to cook indoors, use the wok outside on a charcoal or gas grill. Stir-frys and quick-cooking meals work best; *never deep-fat fry on the grill.*

For a charcoal fire, inside the barbecue firebox arrange *hot* coals in a circle the same size as the wok's cooking ring. Place the wok directly on the coals and proceed as directed in the recipe. Be sure to cover any wooden parts of the wok with several layers of heavy foil, and keep potholders handy at all times.

For a gas grill, follow the manufacturer's directions.

Veal in Cream Sauce *(pictured on pages 14 and 15)*

½ **pound boneless veal** *or* **pork**
1 **tablespoon butter** *or*
   margarine
1 **medium carrot, sliced**
1 **cup sliced fresh mushrooms**
¼ **cup sliced green onion**
½ **cup chicken broth**
¼ **teaspoon salt**
   Dash pepper
½ **cup light cream**
1 **tablespoon all-purpose flour**
   Hot cooked noodles

Partially freeze veal or pork; thinly slice into julienne strips. In wok, melt butter or margarine over medium-high heat. Add veal or pork; stir-fry for 1 minute. Remove from wok. Add carrot, mushrooms, and onion to wok; stir-fry for 3 minutes. Add chicken broth, salt, and pepper; cover and cook about 5 minutes or till carrots are done. Stir cream into flour; stir into vegetable mixture. Cook and stir till thickened and bubbly. Cook and stir 1 minute more. Return meat to wok; heat through. Serve over noodles; garnish with green onion brushes, if desired. Makes 2 or 3 servings.

Spicy Pork Cutlets

1 **pound pork tenderloin**
⅓ **cup Italian salad dressing**
1 **beaten egg**
½ **cup all-purpose flour**
¼ **teaspoon salt**
⅛ **teaspoon pepper**
¾ **cup fine dry bread crumbs**
2 **teaspoons dried parsley flakes**
¼ **teaspoon dried oregano,**
   crushed
   Cooking oil for deep-fat frying

Cut pork crosswise into 6 slices; pound each with meat mallet to ¼-inch thickness. Cut slits around edges to prevent curling. Place in shallow dish; pour dressing over pork. Marinate 30 minutes at room temperature, turning pork twice. Drain, reserving 1 tablespoon dressing. In shallow bowl combine reserved dressing and egg. In a separate bowl mix flour, salt, and pepper. In third bowl mix crumbs, parsley, and oregano. Coat pork slices with flour, then egg, then crumb mixtures.

   In wok heat 1 inch oil to 365°. Fry 1 or 2 slices at a time in hot oil for 2 to 3 minutes. Drain on paper toweling; keep warm. Serve plain or on hamburger buns with lettuce and tomato, if desired. Makes 6 servings.

Sauerkraut-Sausage Supper

½ **pound sausage links***
3 **medium potatoes**
1 **27-ounce can sauerkraut**
1 **medium apple**
2 **tablespoons cooking oil**
1 **medium onion, chopped**
1 **clove garlic, minced**
1 **cup cubed fully cooked ham**
1 **bay leaf**
¾ **teaspoon instant chicken**
   bouillon granules
⅛ **teaspoon pepper**
¾ **cup water**
½ **cup dry white wine**

Slice sausage links diagonally. Peel and thickly slice potatoes. Rinse and drain sauerkraut. Peel, core, and chop the apple.

   Heat wok over medium-high heat; add oil. Stir-fry apple, onion, and garlic in hot oil till onion is tender but not brown. Stir in sausage, potatoes, sauerkraut, ham, bay leaf, bouillon granules, and pepper. Add water and wine. Cover and cook over medium-low heat about 30 minutes or till potatoes are tender, stirring occasionally. Remove bay leaf. Makes 4 servings.

   *Recipe note: Any type of link sausage is suitable for this recipe. Some good choices include Polish sausage, bratwurst, knackwurst, and frankfurters.

BEEF, PORK, and LAMB

Peach and Ham Stir-Fry

½ cup orange juice
1 tablespoon cornstarch
2 tablespoons soy sauce
1 tablespoon sugar
1 tablespoon lemon juice
1 16-ounce can peach slices
2 tablespoons cooking oil
¾ cup peanuts
1 teaspoon grated gingerroot
1 onion, cut into thin wedges
2 zucchini, thinly sliced
2 cups cubed fully cooked ham

Blend orange juice into cornstarch; stir in soy, sugar, and lemon juice. Set aside. Drain peaches; reserve syrup for another use. Heat wok over high heat; add oil. Stir-fry peanuts 2 to 3 minutes or till toasted; remove from wok. Stir-fry gingerroot 30 seconds. Add onion; stir-fry 2 minutes. Add zucchini; stir-fry 1 minute. Remove vegetables from wok; add more oil if needed. Stir-fry ham in hot oil 2 minutes. Stir orange juice mixture; add to wok. Cook and stir till thickened and bubbly; cook and stir 2 minutes more. Stir in peaches, peanuts, and vegetables; cover and cook 1 to 2 minutes. Serve over deep-fried rice sticks, if desired. Serves 6.

Ham and Rice Dinner

2 tablespoons cooking oil
2 stalks celery, bias sliced
1 medium onion, chopped
1 9-ounce package frozen cut
    green beans
1 cup long grain rice
1 16-ounce can tomatoes, cut up
1¼ cups chicken broth
1 teaspoon dried thyme,
    crushed
    Dash bottled hot pepper sauce
1 1½-pound fully cooked ham
    slice, cut into 6 portions

Heat wok over high heat; add oil. Stir-fry celery and onion about 3 minutes or till tender. Stir in beans and rice. Add undrained tomatoes, chicken broth, thyme, and hot pepper sauce; mix well. Bring to boiling; reduce heat. Cover and simmer 15 minutes, stirring occasionally to prevent sticking. Arrange ham portions atop rice mixture. Cover and continue cooking about 10 minutes longer or till rice is tender and ham is heated through. Makes 6 servings.

Pork and Vegetables with Browned Butter

½ teaspoon dry mustard
¼ teaspoon onion powder
¼ teaspoon pepper
1 2-pound smoked pork
    shoulder roll
3 sweet potatoes, peeled and
    sliced 1½ inches thick*
2 10-ounce packages frozen
    brussels sprouts*
½ cup butter or margarine
¼ cup sliced green onion
2 tablespoons lemon juice

Combine mustard, onion powder, and pepper; rub over pork. Pour boiling water into wok to reach ½ inch below steamer rack. Place pork on rack; cover wok and steam 1¼ hours. Arrange potatoes on second steamer rack and place over meat; cover and steam 30 minutes. Add brussels sprouts to potatoes; sprinkle with salt and pepper. Cover and steam 25 minutes or till done. In skillet heat and stir butter and onion till light brown. Stir in lemon juice; spoon over vegetables. Makes 6 servings.

Recipe note: If you have only one steamer rack, use only 2 potatoes and 1 package brussels sprouts. Add vegetables to pork at times indicated above.

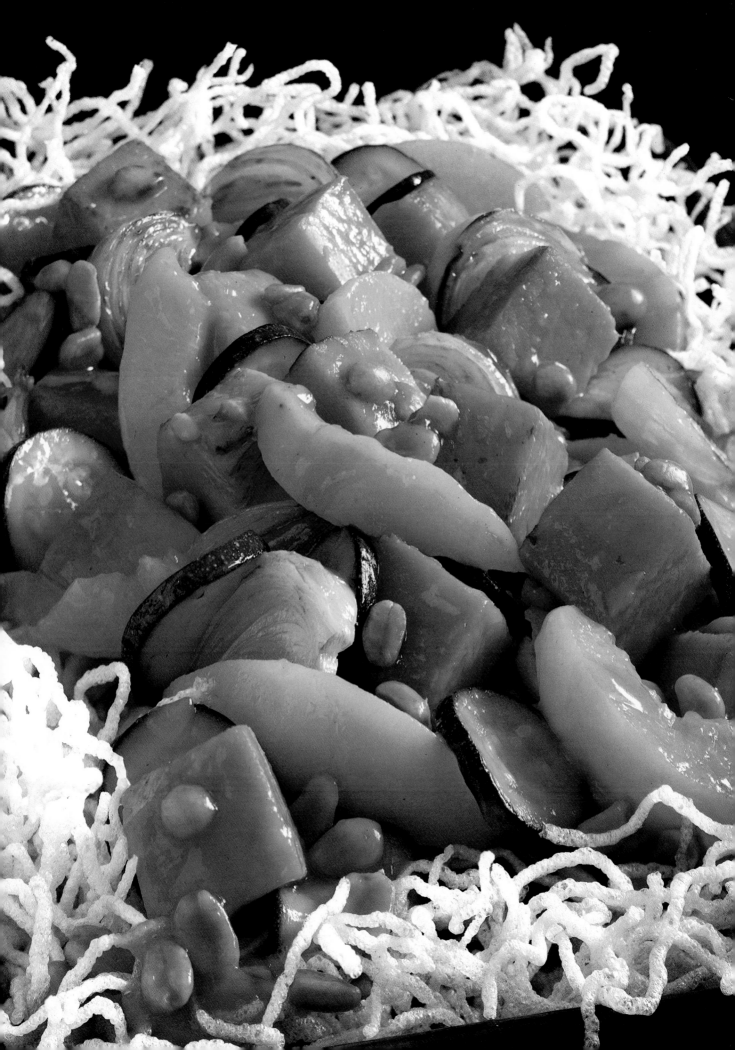

BEEF, PORK, and LAMB

Cucumber Pork

1 pound boneless pork
1 medium cucumber
3 tablespoons soy sauce
1 tablespoon cornstarch
2 tablespoons cold water
1 tablespoon catsup
2 teaspoons sugar
¼ teaspoon bottled hot pepper
    sauce
2 tablespoons cooking oil
2 cloves garlic, minced
1 teaspoon grated gingerroot
2 cups fresh bean sprouts

Partially freeze pork; thinly slice into bite-size strips. Cut cucumber into julienne strips. Blend soy sauce into cornstarch; stir in water, catsup, sugar, and hot pepper sauce. Set aside.

Heat wok over high heat; add oil. Stir-fry garlic and gingerroot for 30 seconds. Add cucumber; stir-fry 30 seconds. Add bean sprouts; stir-fry 1 minute. Remove vegetables from wok. Add more oil if needed. Stir-fry *half* the pork 2 to 3 minutes or till browned; remove. Repeat with remaining pork. Return all pork to wok. Stir soy mixture; stir into pork in wok. Cook and stir till thickened and bubbly; cook and stir 2 minutes more. Return vegetables to wok; cover and cook 1 minute. Makes 4 servings.

Jicama and Pork

1 pound boneless pork
1 medium green pepper
½ cup cold water
2 tablespoons soy sauce
2 tablespoons dry sherry
1 tablespoon cornstarch
2 tablespoons cooking oil
1 clove garlic, minced
1 teaspoon grated gingerroot
1 cup cubed peeled jicama*
1 green onion, sliced
¼ teaspoon salt
3 cups chopped Chinese
    cabbage
    Hot cooked rice

Partially freeze pork; thinly slice into bite-size strips. Cut green pepper into thin strips. Blend water, soy, and sherry into cornstarch; set aside. Heat wok over high heat; add oil. Stir-fry garlic and gingerroot 30 seconds. Stir-fry pork, *half* at a time, 2 to 3 minutes or till browned; remove. Return all meat to wok. Add green pepper, jicama, onion, and salt; stir-fry 1 minute. Add cabbage. Stir soy mixture; stir into meat mixture. Cook and stir till thickened and bubbly; cook and stir 2 minutes longer. Serve with rice. Makes 4 servings.

*Recipe note: Jicama is a crisp root vegetable with a brown skin and white interior. Expect it to remain crisp in this recipe. Popular in Mexico, jicama is available in many supermarkets and specialty shops.

Pork Strips in Cider

1 pound boneless pork
1 tablespoon cooking oil
2 medium onions, chopped
3 medium potatoes, halved and
    sliced
½ teaspoon salt
½ teaspoon ground allspice
    Dash pepper
¾ cup apple cider *or* juice
2 medium apples, peeled and
    sliced
1 teaspoon cornstarch

Partially freeze pork; thinly slice into bite-size strips. Heat wok over high heat; add oil. Brown *half* the pork at a time in hot oil. Remove all from wok. Drain off fat, reserving 1 tablespoon in wok. Add onions to wok; stir-fry over medium-high heat 5 minutes. Add potatoes, salt, allspice, and pepper; stir to combine. Stir in pork. Pour *½ cup* of the cider over all. Cover and simmer for 10 minutes; add apples and simmer 10 minutes longer or till meat and potatoes are tender. Meanwhile, stir together remaining ¼ cup cider and cornstarch. Add to wok; cook and stir till thickened and bubbly. Cook and stir 2 minutes longer. Makes 4 servings.

Fiesta Tostadas *(pictured on pages 14 and 15)*

Cooking oil for deep-fat frying
4 **6-inch corn** *or* **flour tortillas**
1 **pound ground pork, bulk pork sausage, bulk Italian sausage,** *or* **chorizo**
1 **medium onion, chopped**
1 **medium green pepper, chopped**
2 **cloves garlic, minced**
⅓ **cup bottled taco sauce**
½ **teaspoon salt**
 Few dashes bottled hot pepper sauce
2 **cups shredded lettuce**
1 **cup shredded cheddar cheese (4 ounces)**
1 **large avocado, seeded, peeled, and sliced**
1 **small tomato, chopped**
 Bottled taco sauce

In wok heat 1 inch oil to 375°. Fry *one* tortilla at a time for 20 to 40 seconds on each side or till crisp and golden. Drain on paper toweling. Keep warm in 250° oven while preparing meat mixture.

Carefully pour oil from wok. Add pork, onion, green pepper, and garlic to wok. Stir-fry over medium-high heat till pork is done. Drain off fat. Stir in the ⅓ cup taco sauce, the salt, and hot pepper sauce.

To assemble, place a warm tortilla on serving plate; spoon on meat mixture, lettuce, cheese, avocado, and tomato. Top with additional taco sauce, if desired. Makes 4 servings.

Fiesta Tacos: Use ingredients listed above, *except* use *8* tortillas. Heat oil as directed above; fry one tortilla 10 seconds or till limp. With tongs, fold tortilla in half and continue frying, holding edges apart, 1¼ to 1½ minutes longer or till tortilla is crisp. Drain on paper toweling. Repeat with remaining tortillas. Prepare meat mixture as directed above; fill the folded shells.

Hearty Cassoulet

½ **pound bulk pork sausage**
½ **pound boneless pork** *or* **lamb, cut into ½-inch pieces**
1 **medium onion, chopped**
1 **medium stalk celery, chopped**
1 **medium carrot, chopped**
1 **clove garlic, minced**
1 **7½-ounce can tomatoes, cut up**
½ **cup dry white wine** *or* **apple juice**
1 **15-ounce can navy beans, drained**
1 **15-ounce can garbanzo beans, drained**
2 **teaspoons instant beef bouillon granules**
1 **teaspoon dried thyme, crushed**
1 **bay leaf**

Shape sausage into ¾-inch meatballs. In wok stir-fry sausage meatballs on all sides over medium-high heat till brown. Remove from wok, reserving drippings in wok. Add pork or lamb pieces to wok; stir-fry over medium-high heat till meat is lightly browned. Remove from wok, reserving 2 tablespoons drippings in wok (or add cooking oil to wok if necessary). Stir-fry onion, celery, carrot, and garlic in reserved drippings till onion is tender but not brown. Return sausage and pork or lamb to wok. Add *undrained* tomatoes and wine or apple juice. Stir in navy beans, garbanzo beans, bouillon granules, thyme, and bay leaf. Bring to boiling. Cover and cook over low heat for 45 to 60 minutes. Remove bay leaf before serving. Makes 6 servings.

BEEF, PORK, and LAMB

Pepperoni-Vegetable Supper

- **2 slices bacon, cut up**
- **6 ounces pepperoni, sliced ⅛ inch thick**
- **1 small onion, chopped**
- **1 small clove garlic, minced**
- **2 medium potatoes, peeled and cubed**
- **1½ cups Italian-style cooking sauce**
- **½ cup water**
- **1½ cups zucchini cut into julienne strips**
- **1 cup frozen cut green beans**

In wok cook bacon over medium-high heat till crisp; drain, reserving drippings in wok. Set bacon aside. Stir-fry pepperoni, onion, and garlic in reserved drippings till onion is tender but not brown; drain off excess fat. Add potatoes; stir-fry for 3 minutes. Stir in cooking sauce and water; cover and simmer for 20 minutes. Stir in zucchini and beans; cover and simmer 20 minutes longer or till vegetables are tender. To serve, sprinkle with reserved bacon. Makes 4 servings.

Stuffed Grape Leaves

- **1 pound lean ground lamb *or* beef**
- **1 cup cooked rice**
- **¼ cup water**
- **1¼ teaspoons ground cinnamon**
- **1 teaspoon salt**
- **36 grape leaves *or* small cabbage leaves**
- **½ teaspoon salt**
- **¼ cup lemon juice**

In bowl combine meat, rice, water, cinnamon, and 1 teaspoon salt. Rinse grape leaves. (Or for cabbage, cut about 2 inches of heavy center vein from each leaf. Immerse in boiling water 3 minutes or till just limp; drain.) Pat dry with paper toweling. Place about 1 tablespoon meat mixture on wide part of leaf. Fold in bottom edge and sides; roll as for jelly roll. Repeat with remaining leaves and meat mixture. Arrange on steamer rack in wok, seam side down. Pour water into wok to almost cover rolls. Add ½ teaspoon salt. Bring to boiling. Reduce heat; cover and simmer 20 minutes. Add lemon juice; cover and simmer 5 minutes more. Serves 6.

Five-Spice Lamb Stir-Fry

- **1 pound boneless lamb**
- **⅓ cup dry white wine**
- **3 tablespoons teriyaki sauce**
- **1 clove garlic, minced**
- **½ teaspoon five-spice powder**
- **2 teaspoons cornstarch**
- **2 tablespoons cooking oil**
- **6 green onions, bias sliced into 1-inch pieces**
- **Hot cooked rice *or* cellophane noodles**

Partially freeze lamb; thinly slice into bite-size strips. For marinade combine wine, teriyaki sauce, garlic, and five-spice powder. Add lamb, stirring to coat well. Marinate at room temperature 30 minutes (or cover and refrigerate 2 hours). Drain meat, reserving ¼ cup marinade; add water to reserved marinade to make ⅔ cup liquid. Stir into cornstarch; set aside.

Heat wok over high heat; add oil. Stir-fry green onions 1 minute. Remove onions. Stir-fry *half* the lamb at a time for 2 to 3 minutes; remove. Return all lamb to wok. Stir cornstarch mixture; stir into wok. Cook and stir till thickened and bubbly; cook and stir 2 minutes more. Stir in green onions. Cook and stir 1 minute more. Serve over rice or noodles. Makes 4 servings.

Lamb-Eggplant Stew

1 pound boneless lamb
1 large eggplant, peeled
2 tablespoons cooking oil
1 medium onion, chopped
1 clove garlic, minced
1 16-ounce can tomatoes, cut up
1 teaspoon salt
1 teaspoon dried basil, crushed
¼ teaspoon pepper
¼ cup grated Parmesan cheese

Cut lamb and eggplant into ½-inch cubes. Heat wok over high heat; add oil. Stir-fry *half* the lamb at a time in hot oil till browned. Remove all from wok. Stir-fry onion and garlic in wok. Return lamb to wok; stir in *undrained* tomatoes, salt, basil, and pepper. Bring to boiling; reduce heat. Cover and simmer for 20 minutes. Add cubed eggplant; cover and simmer 25 minutes longer or till eggplant and lamb are done. Sprinkle with Parmesan cheese. Makes 4 servings.

Lamb-Lentil Stew

2 tablespoons cooking oil
1 pound boneless lamb, cut into
   1-inch pieces
4 cups beef broth
1 large onion, chopped
3 cloves garlic, minced
2 bay leaves
2 tablespoons tomato paste
1 teaspoon dried oregano,
   crushed
¼ teaspoon salt
   Dash pepper
1 cup dried lentils
2 stalks celery, sliced
2 medium carrots, cut into
   1-inch pieces

Heat wok over high heat; add oil. Stir-fry lamb, *half* at a time, in the hot oil till browned; remove. Drain excess fat from wok. Return all meat to wok; stir in beef broth, onion, garlic, bay leaves, tomato paste, oregano, salt, and pepper. Bring to boiling; reduce heat and simmer, covered, for 30 minutes. Rinse lentils; add to lamb mixture. Stir in celery and carrots. Cover and simmer about 45 minutes more or till lamb and vegetables are done. Remove bay leaves. Makes 6 servings.

Rosemary Lamb Chops

2 tablespoons cooking oil
4 lamb shoulder chops, cut ¾
   inch thick (about 1½ pounds
   total)
1 medium onion, sliced
1 cup sliced fresh mushrooms
½ teaspoon salt
½ teaspoon dried rosemary,
   crushed
¼ teaspoon pepper
½ cup rosé wine *or* beef broth

Heat wok over medium-high heat; add oil. Brown lamb chops on both sides in hot oil; remove from wok. Add onion, mushrooms, salt, rosemary, and pepper to wok. Stir-fry over high heat for 5 minutes. Return chops to wok; pour wine or broth over all. Reduce heat; cover and simmer about 20 minutes or till chops are tender. Arrange chops on serving platter; keep warm. Boil cooking liquid, uncovered, 3 to 4 minutes or till slightly thickened; spoon over chops. Makes 4 servings.

POULTRY

Chicken Veronique

2 **whole large chicken breasts**
2 **tablespoons butter** *or* **margarine**
1 **cup sliced fresh mushrooms**
2 **tablespoons sliced green onion**
⅓ **cup chicken broth**
1 **tablespoon all-purpose flour**
1 **cup seedless grapes, halved**
¼ **cup dry white wine**
  Hot cooked rice

Skin, halve lengthwise, and bone chicken breasts. Cut chicken breasts into 1-inch pieces; set aside. In wok melt butter or margarine over medium-high heat. Stir-fry mushrooms and onions in butter about 2 minutes or till soft. Add chicken pieces and stir-fry about 5 minutes or till chicken is done. Blend chicken broth and flour; add to chicken mixture. Cook and stir till thickened and bubbly; cook and stir 1 minute longer. Stir in grapes and wine; heat through. Serve at once over rice. Makes 4 or 5 servings.

Chicken with Green Peppercorns

2 **whole medium chicken breasts, skinned, halved lengthwise, and boned**
2 **tablespoons butter** *or* **margarine**
1 **small onion, cut into thin wedges**
1 **tablespoon all-purpose flour**
½ **cup light cream**
1 **teaspoon green peppercorns, rinsed and drained,** *or* **freeze-dried green peppercorns***
¼ **teaspoon salt**
¼ **cup dry white wine**

Place chicken between 2 pieces of clear plastic wrap; pound each piece to ¼-inch thickness. Remove wrap; salt lightly. In wok melt butter or margarine over medium heat. Add chicken; cook 4 to 5 minutes on each side or till done. Remove to platter; keep warm. Stir-fry onion till tender but not brown. Blend in flour. Add cream, peppercorns, and salt; cook and stir till thickened and bubbly, crushing peppercorns slightly with spoon. Cook and stir 1 minute more. Stir in wine; heat through. Spoon over chicken. Makes 4 servings.

  *Recipe note: Buy green peppercorns packed in brine or freeze-dried at your supermarket or gourmet specialty shop. Although they are quite different in flavor and texture from black peppercorns, green peppercorns are actually immature berries from the same plant.

Cream Cheese-Stuffed Chicken

1 **3-ounce package cream cheese with chives**
2 **whole small chicken breasts, skinned, halved lengthwise, and boned**
1 **beaten egg**
1 **tablespoon water**
⅓ **cup fine dry bread crumbs**
1 **tablespoon dried parsley flakes**
¼ **cup all-purpose flour**
  Cooking oil for deep-fat frying

Cut cream cheese lengthwise into 4 sticks; chill till ready to use. Meanwhile, place chicken, boned side up, between 2 pieces of clear plastic wrap. Pound chicken out from center with meat mallet to ⅛-inch thickness. Remove wrap. Sprinkle chicken with salt and pepper. Place 1 cheese stick on each piece of chicken. Fold in sides; roll up jelly-roll fashion, pressing ends to seal. Mix egg and water. Mix crumbs and parsley. Coat chicken rolls with flour; dip in egg mixture. Roll in crumb mixture to coat. Cover and chill for 1 hour.

  In wok heat 2 inches cooking oil to 375°. Fry chicken rolls in the hot oil about 5 minutes or till golden brown. Serve at once. Makes 4 servings.

POULTRY

Sesame Chicken and Celery

1 whole large chicken breast
1 tablespoon dry sherry
1 tablespoon soy sauce
2 teaspoons grated gingerroot
¼ cup chicken broth
1 teaspoon cornstarch
2 tablespoons cooking oil
3 stalks celery, bias sliced
4 green onions, bias sliced
Hot cooked rice
2 tablespoons sesame seed, toasted

Skin, halve lengthwise, and bone chicken; cut into 1-inch pieces. Place in small bowl. Add sherry, soy, and gingerroot; stir to coat. Let stand at room temperature 20 minutes. Stir broth into cornstarch; set aside.

Heat wok over high heat; add oil. Stir-fry celery and onions 2 minutes or till crisp-tender; remove. Add more oil if needed. Drain chicken, reserving soy mixture. Stir-fry chicken 3 minutes or till just browned. Add soy mixture to broth mixture; stir into wok. Cook and stir till thickened and bubbly; cook and stir 2 minutes more. Stir in vegetables. Cover and cook 1 minute. Spoon over rice; sprinkle with sesame seed. Makes 2 or 3 servings.

Chicken in Mustard Sauce

6 chicken thighs
¼ cup snipped chives
3 tablespoons all-purpose flour
2 tablespoons butter
½ cup dry white wine
½ cup whipping cream
2 tablespoons Dijon-style mustard
Hot cooked wild rice *or* long grain rice

Make a lengthwise slit in each thigh and cut out the bone. Sprinkle inside with chives, salt, and pepper. Fold to original shape; secure with wooden picks. Coat chicken with flour. In wok melt butter over medium-high heat. Add chicken; brown about 5 minutes on each side. Add wine; cover and simmer over low heat 30 minutes or till done. Remove chicken. Skim fat from pan juices. Stir cream and mustard into juices; cook and stir till smooth and slightly thickened. Return chicken to wok; heat through. Serve over rice. Makes 3 servings.

Boning Chicken Breasts

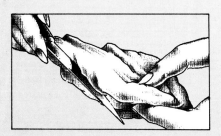

Save money by boning chicken breasts at home. First, remove the skin simply by pulling it away from the meat with your fingers. Using a large heavy knife or a cleaver, split the breast in half lengthwise. Place breast half, bone side down, on work surface. Starting from the breastbone side, cut meat away from bone using a thin, sharp knife, as shown. Cut as close to the bone as possible, using a sawing motion and pressing the flat side of the knife against the rib bones. As you cut, gently pull the meat up and away from the bones. Save the bones for making chicken stock, or discard them.

Oriental Chicken

- **1 whole medium chicken breast**
- **2 tablespoons soy sauce**
- **1 tablespoon cornstarch**
- **⅓ cup chicken broth**
- **2 tablespoons dry sherry**
- **¼ teaspoon sugar**
- **2 tablespoons cooking oil**
- **1 cup sliced fresh mushrooms**
- **1 8½-ounce can sliced bamboo shoots, drained**
- **1 6-ounce package frozen pea pods, thawed**

Skin, halve lengthwise, and bone chicken breast; thinly slice chicken into bite-size pieces. Stir soy sauce into cornstarch; stir in chicken broth, sherry, sugar, and ¼ teaspoon *pepper*. Set aside.

Heat wok over high heat; add oil. Stir-fry mushrooms and bamboo shoots 1 minute. Remove from wok. Add pea pods; stir-fry 1 minute. Remove from wok. Add more oil to wok if needed. Stir-fry chicken 2 to 3 minutes or till done. Stir broth mixture; stir into wok. Cook and stir till thickened and bubbly; cook and stir 2 minutes more. Return all vegetables to wok; cover and cook 2 minutes. Serve over hot cooked rice, if desired. Makes 2 or 3 servings.

Rosamarina Chicken Stir-Fry

- **2 whole medium chicken breasts**
- **2 small green peppers**
- **1 cup rosamarina *or* ditalini***
- **2 tablespoons cooking oil**
- **1 medium onion, sliced**
- **½ teaspoon ground cumin**
- **½ teaspoon ground red pepper**
- **1 8-ounce can whole kernel corn, drained**
- **¼ cup chopped canned green chili peppers**
- **¾ teaspoon salt**
- **2 tomatoes, peeled and chopped**
- **1 cup shredded cheddar cheese**

Skin, halve lengthwise, and bone chicken breasts; cut into ½-inch cubes. Cut peppers into strips. Cook pasta according to package directions; drain. Meanwhile, heat wok over high heat; add oil. Stir-fry chicken 3 minutes or till lightly browned. Add green peppers, onion, cumin, and red pepper; stir-fry 3 minutes, adding more oil if needed. Stir in drained pasta, corn, chili peppers, and salt. Cover and cook 2 minutes or till hot. Stir in tomatoes; sprinkle with cheese. Cover and cook 2 minutes or till cheese melts. Makes 4 servings.

*Recipe note: Rosamarina and ditalini are kinds of pasta. Rosamarina is rice-shaped, and ditalini is shaped like tiny thimbles. If they are unavailable at your supermarket, visit a specialty food shop or substitute another very small pasta.

Plum-Sauced Chicken

- **⅓ cup plum preserves**
- **¼ cup finely chopped onion**
- **2 tablespoons frozen orange juice concentrate**
- **2 teaspoons instant chicken bouillon granules**
- **½ teaspoon ground allspice**
- **½ teaspoon Kitchen Bouquet**
- **1 2½- to 3-pound broiler-fryer chicken, cut up**
- **1 tablespoon cold water**
- **4 teaspoons cornstarch**
- **Hot cooked rice**

In bowl combine first 6 ingredients. Sprinkle chicken with salt and pepper; place in 8x1½-inch round baking dish. Pour plum mixture atop; cover with foil.

Pour boiling water into wok to reach ½ inch below steamer rack. Place baking dish on rack. Cover wok and steam 50 minutes or till tender. Remove chicken to platter; keep warm. Skim excess fat from mixture in dish. Measure plum mixture; add water if needed to make 1¼ cups liquid. In saucepan stir 1 tablespoon cold water into cornstarch. Stir in plum liquid. Cook and stir till thickened and bubbly; cook and stir 2 minutes more. Spoon some sauce atop chicken; pass remainder. Serve with rice. Makes 6 servings.

Festive Chicken *(pictured also on the cover)*

2 tablespoons cooking oil
1 medium onion, chopped
1 small green pepper, cut into
   strips
1 clove garlic, minced
2 teaspoons curry powder
½ teaspoon dried thyme,
   crushed
¼ teaspoon ground cloves
1 16-ounce can tomatoes, cut up
¼ cup dried currants
½ teaspoon salt
1 2½- to 3-pound broiler-fryer
   chicken, cut up
¼ cup sliced almonds, toasted
   Hot cooked rice

Heat wok over high heat; add oil. Stir-fry onion, green pepper, and garlic for 3 to 5 minutes or till onion is tender. Add curry, thyme, and cloves; stir-fry 2 minutes longer. Stir in *undrained* tomatoes, currants, and salt. Add chicken pieces, spooning tomato mixture over chicken. Bring to boiling; reduce heat. Cover and simmer for 35 to 40 minutes or till chicken is tender. Remove chicken. Boil sauce, uncovered, about 10 minutes or till reduced to desired consistency. Skim off fat. Return chicken to wok; heat through. Garnish with almonds. Serve with rice. Makes 4 to 6 servings.

Chicken Luau

1¼ cups milk
1 3½-ounce can shredded
   coconut
¼ cup cooking oil
1 2½- to 3-pound broiler-fryer
   chicken, cut up
1 large onion, chopped
1 13¾-ounce can chicken broth
3 medium sweet potatoes,
   peeled and sliced ½ inch
   thick
1 pound fresh spinach, chopped
2 tablespoons cornstarch

In saucepan heat milk just to boiling. Add coconut and simmer 5 minutes. Strain milk, pressing coconut against side of strainer. Discard coconut; let milk cool.
   Heat wok over medium heat; add oil. Brown chicken pieces in hot oil on all sides. Add onion; cook till tender. Add broth and 1 teaspoon *salt.* Cover and simmer for 15 minutes. Add potatoes; simmer, covered, 25 minutes or till chicken and potatoes are tender. Top with spinach; sprinkle with ½ teaspoon *salt.* Cover and simmer 5 minutes or till spinach is done. Remove spinach, potatoes, and chicken. Stir cooled milk into cornstarch; stir into pan juices. Cook and stir till thickened and bubbly; cook and stir 2 minutes more. Return chicken and vegetables to wok; heat through. Makes 4 to 6 servings.

Apricot-Glazed Cornish Hens

2 1- to 1½-pound Cornish game
   hens, halved lengthwise
¼ cup cooking oil
⅓ cup water
3 tablespoons lemon juice
1 tablespoon soy sauce
½ teaspoon ground ginger
¼ cup apricot preserves

Thaw hens, if frozen. Heat wok over high heat; add oil. Brown hens in oil about 10 minutes, turning often. Drain off fat. Add water, lemon juice, soy sauce, and ginger to wok. Cover and simmer 40 to 45 minutes or till done, turning hens once or twice. Remove hens from wok; keep warm. Skim fat from liquid. Boil liquid, uncovered, till reduced to ½ cup. Stir in preserves; heat through. Pour over birds. Makes 4 servings.

Festive Chicken

POULTRY

Chili Chicken and Spaghetti

1 tablespoon butter *or*
    margarine
1 medium onion, chopped
1 medium carrot, thinly sliced
    (½ cup)
1 teaspoon chili powder
1 2½- to 3-pound broiler-fryer
    chicken, cut up
1 cup tomato juice
1 teaspoon finely shredded
    lemon peel
1 tablespoon lemon juice
1 teaspoon salt
½ teaspoon sugar
¼ teaspoon pepper
2 tablespoons cold water
1 tablespoon cornstarch
    Hot cooked spaghetti

In wok melt butter or margarine over medium-high heat. Add onion; stir-fry till tender but not brown. Stir in carrot and chili powder. Arrange chicken in wok; add tomato juice, lemon peel, lemon juice, salt, sugar, and pepper.

Bring mixture to boiling; reduce heat. Cover and simmer 45 to 50 minutes or till chicken is tender. Remove chicken to platter; keep warm. Skim fat from pan juices. Combine water and cornstarch; stir into pan juices. Cook and stir till thickened and bubbly; cook and stir 2 minutes longer. Spoon some of the sauce over chicken; pass remainder. Serve with hot cooked spaghetti. Makes 6 servings.

Turkey Croquettes with Dill Sauce

1 tablespoon cooking oil
1 pound ground raw turkey
3 tablespoons butter *or*
    margarine
¼ cup all-purpose flour
¾ cup milk
1 teaspoon grated onion
2 tablespoons butter *or*
    margarine
2 tablespoons all-purpose flour
1 tablespoon prepared mustard
½ teaspoon salt
½ teaspoon dried dillweed
    Dash ground nutmeg
    Dash pepper
1¼ cups milk
1 hard-cooked egg, chopped
½ cup fine dry bread crumbs
1 beaten egg
2 tablespoons water
    Cooking oil for deep-fat frying

Heat wok over medium-high heat; add 1 tablespoon oil. Cook turkey in hot oil till done, stirring constantly to break meat into fine pieces; drain off fat.

In 1-quart saucepan melt 3 tablespoons butter or margarine; stir in ¼ cup flour. Add ¾ cup milk all at once; cook and stir till thickened and bubbly. Cook and stir 1 minute longer. Stir in cooked turkey and grated onion. Cover and chill thoroughly.

To prepare dill sauce, in small saucepan melt 2 tablespoons butter or margarine. Stir in 2 tablespoons flour, the mustard, salt, dillweed, nutmeg, and pepper. Stir in 1¼ cups milk all at once. Cook and stir till thickened and bubbly; cook and stir 1 minute longer. Stir in the chopped egg; heat through but *do not boil*. Cover and keep warm while frying croquettes.

Divide chilled turkey mixture into 12 equal portions; shape into balls. Roll balls in bread crumbs; shape into cones by rolling with palms of hands. Dip cones into a mixture of the beaten egg and water to coat; roll in bread crumbs again.

Wipe out wok; in wok heat 2 inches oil to 365°. Fry 3 or 4 croquettes at a time for 1½ to 2 minutes or till heated through, turning once. Drain on paper toweling; keep warm in oven till all are cooked. Serve with the dill sauce. Makes 4 to 6 servings.

Meat Croquettes: Prepare Turkey Croquettes with Dill Sauce as directed above, *except* substitute 1 pound *ground beef, pork, lamb,* or *veal* for the turkey.

Curried Chicken and Rice

1 2½- to 3-pound broiler-fryer
   chicken, cut up
2½ cups water
1 medium onion, chopped
1 tablespoon curry powder
1¼ cups long grain rice
¼ cup snipped dried apricots
1 teaspoon instant chicken
   bouillon granules
½ teaspoon salt
¼ cup peanuts *or* cashews
   Paprika

Sprinkle chicken pieces lightly with salt and pepper. In wok combine chicken, water, onion, and curry powder. Bring to boiling; reduce heat. Cover and simmer 20 minutes. Skim excess fat from cooking liquid. Stir rice, apricots, chicken bouillon granules, and salt into chicken in wok. Return to boiling. Reduce heat; cover and simmer 20 minutes more or till rice and chicken are done. Sprinkle with peanuts or cashews and paprika. Makes 6 servings.

Apples with Chicken Livers

½ cup apple juice
2 teaspoons cornstarch
½ teaspoon salt
¼ teaspoon dried rosemary,
   crushed
2 tablespoons cooking oil
2 medium apples, cored and cut
   into thin wedges
1 medium onion, sliced
1 pound chicken livers, halved
2 tablespoons slivered almonds,
   toasted

Stir together apple juice, cornstarch, salt, and rosemary; set aside. Heat wok over high heat; add oil. Add apples; cook, stirring often, till apples are tender. Remove apples from wok. Add onion to wok; stir-fry till onion is tender but not brown. Remove from wok. Add more oil if necessary. Stir-fry livers about 5 minutes or till done. Stir apple juice mixture; stir into livers. Cook and stir till thickened and bubbly; cook and stir 2 minutes longer. Stir apples, onion, and almonds into liver mixture. Cover and cook 2 to 3 minutes or till heated through. Makes 4 servings.

Sherried Duckling

1 4- to 5-pound fresh *or* frozen
   duckling, quartered, *or* two
   1¼-pound Cornish game
   hens, halved lengthwise
1 tablespoon cooking oil
⅔ cup chicken broth
¼ cup dry sherry
2 tablespoons sliced green
   onion
1 teaspoon fines herbs
1 bay leaf
   Dash pepper
2 tablespoons cold water
4 teaspoons cornstarch
   Hot cooked rice

Thaw duckling or hens, if frozen. Heat wok over medium-high heat; add oil. Brown duckling or Cornish hen pieces on all sides about 15 minutes. Drain off all the fat. Add broth, sherry, green onion, fines herbs, bay leaf, and pepper. Cover and simmer duckling for 45 to 50 minutes (simmer hens for 35 to 40 minutes) or till tender. Remove birds to platter; keep warm. Discard bay leaf. Skim fat from pan juices. Measure juices; add water, if necessary, to make 1¼ cups liquid. Return to wok. Stir 2 tablespoons cold water into cornstarch; add to liquid in wok. Cook and stir till thickened and bubbly; cook and stir 2 minutes more. Pour some sauce over duckling; pass remainder. Serve with rice. Makes 4 servings.

Broccoli and Fish Bundles *(pictured on the cover)*

4 fresh *or* frozen fish fillets
1 10-ounce package frozen broccoli spears
2 small carrots, quartered lengthwise
1 tablespoon butter *or* margarine
½ teaspoon dried dillweed
¼ teaspoon salt
2 lemon slices, halved
¼ cup whipping cream
¼ cup mayonnaise

Thaw fish, if frozen. In saucepan cook broccoli and carrots in small amount of boiling water about 5 minutes or till crisp-tender; drain. Dot fish fillets with butter or margarine; sprinkle with dill and salt. Place broccoli and carrots across fish fillets; roll up fish around vegetables and fasten with wooden picks.

Pour boiling water into wok to reach ½ inch below steamer rack. Arrange fillets on rack; top each with a half lemon slice. Cover wok and steam 12 to 15 minutes or till fish flakes easily when tested with a fork. Meanwhile, whip cream till soft peaks form; fold in mayonnaise. Pass sauce with fish. Makes 4 servings.

Fish Rolls Florentine

4 fresh *or* frozen fish fillets
1 10-ounce package frozen chopped spinach
1 3-ounce package cream cheese, softened
1 tablespoon minced dried onion
2 teaspoons lemon juice
1 7½-ounce can semi-condensed savory cream of mushroom soup
¼ teaspoon dried basil, crushed

Thaw fish, if frozen. Thaw spinach and drain well. Combine spinach, cream cheese, onion, and lemon juice; mix well. Spread ¼ of the spinach mixture on each fillet. Roll up each fillet jelly-roll style, starting with the short end; secure with wooden picks. In wok combine soup and basil. Heat to simmering. Add fish rolls, spooning some sauce over fish. Cover and simmer over medium-low heat 15 to 20 minutes or till fish flakes easily when tested with a fork. Remove to serving plate; spoon some sauce over fish. Pass remainder. Makes 4 servings.

Recipe note: For easy roll-ups, use thin fillets such as sole or flounder, about 4 ounces each.

Sweet-Sour Fish and Cherries

1 12-ounce package frozen batter-fried fish portions
1 tablespoon cooking oil
1 medium carrot, sliced
3 green onions, sliced
1 clove garlic, minced
¾ cup chicken broth
¼ cup honey
3 tablespoons vinegar
1½ teaspoons soy sauce
1 small green pepper
1 tablespoon cornstarch
1 cup fresh *or* frozen pitted tart red cherries

Cook fish portions according to package directions; keep warm. Heat wok over high heat; add oil. Stir-fry carrot, green onions, and garlic for 3 minutes. Stir in broth, honey, vinegar, and soy sauce. Bring to boiling; reduce heat. Cover and simmer about 10 minutes or till carrot is nearly tender. Cut green pepper into ½-inch squares; add to wok. Simmer 1 minute. Combine 2 tablespoons cold *water* and the cornstarch; stir into wok. Cook and stir till thickened and bubbly; cook and stir 2 minutes longer. Stir in cherries; heat through. Arrange hot fish portions on platter; top with cherry sauce. Makes 4 servings.

Sweet-Sour Fish and Cherries

FISH and SEAFOOD

Steamed Salmon with Parsley Butter *(pictured on page 40)*

4 fresh *or* frozen salmon *or*
    other fish steaks, cut 1 inch
    thick
4 lemon *or* lime slices
¼ cup butter *or* margarine,
    softened
2 tablespoons snipped parsley
1 tablespoon sliced green onion
    or chopped shallot

Thaw fish, if frozen. Top each steak with a lemon or lime slice; sprinkle with salt and pepper. Pour boiling water into wok to reach ½ inch below steamer rack. Place fish on steamer rack. Cover wok and steam for 10 to 12 minutes or till fish flakes easily when tested with a fork. Remove to platter.

    Meanwhile, stir together the softened butter or margarine, the parsley, and onion or shallot till well combined. Spoon about *1 tablespoon* of the butter mixture onto *each* fish steak. Garnish with lemon or lime slices and green onion brushes, if desired. Makes 4 servings.

Orange Steamed Fish

1 pound fresh *or* frozen fish
    fillets
2 tablespoons cooking oil
1 medium onion, chopped
2 cloves garlic, minced
½ teaspoon grated gingerroot
¼ cup frozen orange juice
    concentrate
2 tablespoons snipped parsley
1 tablespoon soy sauce
⅛ teaspoon pepper
    Hot cooked rice

Thaw fish, if frozen. Arrange fish in heatproof serving dish. Heat wok over high heat; add oil. Stir-fry onion, garlic, and gingerroot in hot oil 5 minutes. Stir in juice concentrate, parsley, soy sauce, and pepper; bring to boiling. Pour mixture over fish.

    Wipe out wok. Add boiling water to wok to reach ½ inch below steamer rack. Place serving dish with fish on steamer rack. Cover wok and steam about 10 minutes or till fish flakes easily when tested with a fork. Serve with hot cooked rice. Makes 4 servings.

    Recipe note: Be sure dish doesn't cover all the holes in steamer rack, so steam can circulate around fish.

Fish Ratatouille

1 pound fresh *or* frozen fish
    fillets
2 tablespoons cooking oil
1 medium onion, thinly sliced
1 medium green pepper,
    chopped
1 clove garlic, minced
1 eggplant, peeled and cubed
1 7½-ounce can tomatoes, cut
    up
1 tablespoon snipped parsley
1 teaspoon dried basil, crushed
½ teaspoon salt
½ teaspoon sugar
⅛ teaspoon pepper
¼ cup grated Parmesan cheese

Thaw fish, if frozen. Cut fish into cubes. Heat wok over high heat; add oil. Stir-fry onion, green pepper, and garlic for 3 minutes. Add eggplant; stir-fry 5 minutes. Stir in *undrained* tomatoes, parsley, basil, salt, sugar, and pepper. Carefully stir in fish cubes. Cover and cook over low heat about 20 minutes or till fish flakes easily when tested with a fork, stirring occasionally. Sprinkle with Parmesan. Makes 4 servings.

Clam and Cheese Spaghetti

1 pint shucked clams *or* two 6½-
   ounce cans minced clams
1 tablespoon cooking oil
3 green onions, thinly sliced
1 clove garlic, minced
1 tablespoon all-purpose flour
1 cup milk
2 tablespoons snipped parsley
½ teaspoon salt
½ teaspoon dried basil, crushed
   Dash pepper
8 ounces spaghetti *or* linguine,
   cooked and drained
¼ cup grated Parmesan cheese

Drain clams, reserving ½ cup liquid. Cut up any large clams. Heat wok over high heat; add oil. Stir-fry green onions and garlic for 2 minutes. Stir in flour. Add milk and reserved clam liquid. Cook and stir over medium-high heat till slightly thickened and bubbly; cook and stir 1 minute longer. Stir in clams, parsley, salt, basil, and pepper. Cook and stir 2 minutes longer or till clams are heated through. Add spaghetti and cheese to wok; toss to combine and heat through. Pass additional grated Parmesan cheese, if desired. Makes 4 or 5 servings.

Steamer Meals

Prepare two or three separate dishes on just one burner by stacking steamer racks over boiling water in your wok. Use multilayered aluminum or bamboo steamer racks that fit together tightly. Place your main dish on one rack and vegetables on one or two others for a complete meal. Don't overcrowd any of the racks because steam must circulate through all levels.

Place the food requiring the longest cooking time on the bottom, then add the remaining racks at intervals so all the foods will be done at the same time; there's no need to add extra time for extra racks.

Check the Steamed Vegetable Chart on page 60 to find timings for steam-cooking many vegetables. Refer to the index for more recipes.

Oriental Fish and Green Beans

1 16-ounce package frozen haddock *or* other fish fillets
1 9-ounce package frozen French-style green beans
2 tablespoons soy sauce
1 tablespoon cornstarch
¼ cup chicken broth
2 teaspoons sugar
2 teaspoons vinegar
½ teaspoon ground ginger
4 tablespoons cooking oil
2 green onions, sliced

Thaw fish and green beans; cut fish into 1-inch cubes. Stir soy sauce into cornstarch; stir in broth, sugar, vinegar, and ginger. Set aside.

Heat wok over high heat; add *2 tablespoons* of the oil. Stir-fry beans and onions 3 minutes; remove from wok. Add the remaining oil to wok. Add fish; cook over medium-high heat, stirring occasionally, for 4 to 5 minutes or till fish flakes easily when tested with a fork. Stir soy mixture; stir into fish. Cook and stir till thickened and bubbly; cook and stir 2 minutes longer. Stir in beans and onions. Cook 1 to 2 minutes more. Makes 4 servings.

Scallops with Apples and Pea Pods

12 ounces fresh *or* frozen scallops
¼ cup apple juice *or* cider
2 teaspoons cornstarch
1 tablespoon soy sauce
2 tablespoons cooking oil
3 small apples, cored and sliced
1 medium onion, chopped
1 6-ounce package frozen pea pods, thawed

Thaw scallops, if frozen. Cut up any large scallops. Stir apple juice into cornstarch; stir in soy sauce. Set aside. Heat wok over high heat; add *1 tablespoon* of the oil. Stir-fry apples and onion 3 minutes or till just tender; remove from wok. Add remaining oil to wok. Stir-fry scallops 4 to 5 minutes or till done. Stir soy mixture; add to scallops. Cook and stir till thickened and bubbly; cook and stir 2 minutes more. Stir pea pods into scallop mixture; stir in apples and onion. Cover and cook 1 to 2 minutes or till pea pods are done. Makes 4 servings.

Red Shrimp with Linguine

8 ounces fresh *or* frozen shelled shrimp
⅓ cup dry white wine
2 teaspoons cornstarch
1 8-ounce can tomato sauce
2 tablespoons butter *or* margarine
¼ cup chopped onion
½ medium green pepper, cut into strips
1 clove garlic, minced
4 anchovy fillets
¼ cup snipped parsley
6 ounces linguine, cooked and drained

Thaw shrimp, if frozen. In small bowl stir wine into cornstarch. Stir in tomato sauce; set aside.

In wok melt butter or margarine over medium-high heat. Stir-fry onion, green pepper and garlic for 1 minute or till vegetables are hot. Add shrimp; stir-fry 7 to 8 minutes longer or till shrimp are done. Remove mixture from wok. Add anchovies to wok, mashing with back of spoon. Stir tomato mixture; add to anchovies. Cook and stir till thickened and bubbly; cook and stir 2 minutes longer.

Return shrimp mixture to wok; stir in snipped parsley. Cook and stir 1 minute more or till hot. Serve over hot cooked linguine. Makes 2 or 3 servings.

Scallops with Apples and Pea Pods; Steamed Salmon with Parsley Butter (see recipe, page 38)

FISH and SEAFOOD

Tempura

¼ **pound fresh *or* frozen halibut *or* other fish steaks**
½ **pound fresh *or* frozen scallops**
   Tempura Sauce
   Sweet-Sour Sauce
½ **pound fresh broccoli**
¼ **pound fresh green beans**
1 **sweet potato, peeled**
1 **medium onion**
¼ **pound whole fresh mushrooms**
½ **pound chicken breast, skinned and boned**
1 **egg**
¾ **cup ice water**
1 **cup all-purpose flour**
1 **tablespoon cooking oil**
½ **teaspoon sugar**
½ **teaspoon salt**
   Ice cubes
   Cooking oil for deep-fat frying

Thaw fish and scallops, if frozen. Prepare the sauces; set aside. Cut broccoli into bite-size pieces. Cut beans into 2-inch lengths. Slice sweet potato ½ inch thick. Cut onion into slices and separate into rings. Halve large mushrooms and scallops. Cut fish and chicken into 1-inch pieces. In bowl beat egg with rotary beater; add ice water. Beat in flour, 1 tablespoon oil, the sugar, and salt just till moistened. Add 1 or 2 ice cubes to bowl; use batter immediately.

In wok heat 1½ inches cooking oil to 400°. Add 1 teaspoon *salt*. Spear fish, chicken, or vegetable pieces with fondue forks; swirl in batter to coat. Fry in hot oil for 2 to 3 minutes. Pass sauces; serve with hot cooked rice, if desired. Makes 8 servings.

Tempura Sauce: In saucepan mix ½ cup *water*, ¼ cup *soy sauce*, 2 tablespoons dry *sherry*, ½ teaspoon instant *chicken bouillon granules*, and ½ teaspoon *sugar*; bring to boiling. Keep warm.

Sweet-Sour Sauce: In saucepan mix ½ cup packed *brown sugar* and 1 tablespoon *cornstarch*. Stir in ⅓ cup *vinegar*, ⅓ cup *chicken broth*, 1 tablespoon *soy sauce*, ¼ teaspoon *garlic powder*, and ¼ teaspoon ground *ginger*. Cook and stir till thickened and bubbly; cook and stir 2 minutes more. Keep warm.

Paella *(pictured on pages 14 and 15)*

12 **small clams in shells**
 8 **ounces chorizo *or* Italian sausage links**
 1 **2½- to 3-pound broiler-fryer chicken, cut up**
 1 **medium onion, chopped**
 1 **medium green pepper, chopped**
 1 **stalk celery with leaves, chopped**
 2 **cloves garlic, minced**
 1 **cup long grain rice**
 2 **large tomatoes, peeled and chopped**
 1 **bay leaf**
1½ **teaspoons salt**
 ½ **teapoon dried oregano, crushed**
 ¼ **teaspoon thread saffron, crushed**
 2 **cups water**
12 **ounces fresh *or* frozen shelled shrimp**
 1 **10-ounce package frozen peas**

Cover clams in shells with salted water using 3 tablespoons salt to 8 cups cold water; let stand 15 minutes. Rinse. Repeat soaking and rinsing twice. Cut sausage into 1-inch pieces.

Heat wok over medium-high heat. Add sausage; stir-fry till brown on all sides. Remove sausage, reserving drippings in wok. Brown chicken in drippings about 10 minutes, turning often. Remove from wok, reserving drippings.

Stir-fry onion, green pepper, celery, and garlic about 5 minutes or till onion is tender. Stir in uncooked rice, tomatoes, bay leaf, salt, oregano, and saffron; stir-fry 1 minute. Add chicken and water; cover and simmer for 20 minutes, stirring once. Add shrimp, peas, clams, and cooked sausage. Cover and simmer about 15 minutes or till clams open and chicken and rice are done. Makes 8 servings.

Fried Oysters

1 pint shucked oysters
1 beaten egg
1 tablespoon milk
½ cup all-purpose flour
½ cup yellow cornmeal
½ teaspoon onion salt
  Dash pepper
  Cooking oil for deep-fat frying
  Tartar sauce
  Lemon wedges

Drain oysters; pat dry with paper toweling. Stir together egg and milk. In another bowl combine flour, cornmeal, onion salt, and pepper. Dip each oyster in egg mixture, then roll in cornmeal mixture to coat.

In wok heat 1½ inches oil to 365°. Add oysters a few at a time; cook 2 to 3 minutes or till golden. Drain on paper toweling; keep warm in oven while frying remainder. Serve with tartar sauce and lemon wedges. Makes 4 to 6 servings.

Crispy Fish Nuggets: Cut 1 pound fresh *or* thawed, frozen *fish fillets* into 1-inch pieces. Prepare as directed above.

Crab Cakes

1 beaten egg
¾ cup soft bread crumbs
2 tablespooons mayonnaise
¾ teaspoon dry mustard
⅛ teaspoon bottled hot pepper
  sauce
1 7-ounce can crab meat,
  drained, flaked, and
  cartilage removed
2 tablespoons snipped parsley
1 beaten egg
1 tablespoon water
¾ cup finely crushed saltine
  crackers (21 crackers)
  Cooking oil for deep-fat frying

In bowl combine 1 egg, bread crumbs, mayonnaise, mustard, and hot pepper sauce. Stir in crab meat and parsley. Using about ¼ cup crab mixture for each, shape into patties. Cover and chill 1 hour. In small bowl combine 1 egg and water. Dip patties in crushed crackers, then in egg-water mixture; coat with crushed crackers again.

In wok heat 1½ inches cooking oil to 375°. Fry 2 or 3 patties at a time for 2 to 3 minutes or till golden on both sides. Drain on paper toweling. Serve with cocktail sauce, if desired. Makes 3 servings.

Tuna Cakes: Prepare Crab Cakes as above, *except* substitute one 6½-ounce can *tuna*, drained and flaked, for the crab meat. Serve with tartar sauce, if desired.

Salt Cod Cakes

8 ounces salt cod
3 cups chopped peeled potatoes
1 beaten egg
2 tablespoons butter *or*
  margarine
⅛ teaspoon pepper
¾ cup finely crushed saltine
  crackers (21 crackers)
  Cooking oil for deep-fat frying
  Lemon wedges

Soak salt cod in enough cold water to cover for 12 hours, changing water once. Drain well. Chop the cod. In covered saucepan cook cod and potatoes in a large amount of boiling water for 15 minutes; drain. In mixer bowl beat cod and potatoes with electric mixer till well mashed. Add egg, butter or margarine, and pepper; beat well. Using about ¼ cup cod mixture for each, shape into ½-inch-thick cakes. Coat with crushed crackers.

In wok heat 1½ inches oil to 375°. Fry a few cakes at a time for 2 minutes; turn and fry 1 to 2 minutes longer or till golden. Drain on paper toweling. Serve with lemon wedges; garnish with parsley, if desired. Makes 4 servings.

MEATLESS DISHES

Minestrone Stir-Fry

4 ounces spaghetti
2 tablespoons cooking oil
2 carrots, thinly sliced
1 medium onion, chopped
1 stalk celery, sliced
1 clove garlic, minced
2 cups chopped cabbage
2 zucchini, thinly sliced
1 20-ounce can cannelini*
1 8-ounce can tomato sauce
1 teaspoon dried basil, crushed
¼ cup grated Parmesan cheese

Cook spaghetti according to package directions; drain well and keep warm. Meanwhile, heat wok over high heat; add oil. Stir-fry carrots, onion, celery, and garlic 5 minutes. Stir cabbage, zucchini, *undrained* beans, tomato sauce, and basil into wok. Bring to boiling; reduce heat. Cover and simmer 8 to 10 minutes or till vegetables are crisp-tender, stirring occasionally. Add spaghetti to wok; toss gently. Sprinkle with cheese and snipped parsley, if desired. Makes 4 servings.

Recipe note: Cannelini is another name for white kidney beans. If these are not available, use one 16-ounce can navy beans in this recipe.

Vegetable Stir-Fry

2 medium carrots
2 cups green beans
2 cups sliced cauliflower
4 teaspoons cornstarch
⅓ cup soy sauce
⅓ cup orange juice
2 teaspoons sugar
2 tablespoons cooking oil
1 cup sliced fresh mushrooms
1¼ cups peanuts (5 ounces)
2 cups hot cooked rice
2 tablespoons sesame seed, toasted

Cut carrots into julienne strips. Bias-slice green beans into 1-inch lengths. In saucepan cook carrots and beans, uncovered, in boiling salted water for 3 minutes. Add cauliflower; cook, covered, 2 minutes more. Drain well. In bowl stir ½ cup cold *water* into the cornstarch; stir in soy sauce, orange juice, sugar, and ¼ teaspoon *pepper*. Set aside.

Heat wok over high heat; add oil. Stir-fry carrots, beans, cauliflower, and mushrooms 2 minutes or till crisp-tender. Add peanuts; stir-fry 30 seconds more. Stir soy mixture; stir into wok. Cook and stir till thickened and bubbly; cook and stir 2 minutes more. Serve over rice; top with sesame seed. Makes 4 servings.

Tofu-Vegetable Stir-Fry

8 ounces tofu (bean curd)
2 tablespoons soy sauce
1 tablespoon cornstarch
½ teaspoon sugar
2 tablespoons cooking oil
1 teaspoon grated gingerroot
2 carrots, thinly sliced
1 medium onion, sliced
1 cup thinly sliced cauliflower
1 cup frozen peas
½ cup broken walnuts
2 cups hot cooked rice

Cut tofu into ½-inch cubes. Stir soy sauce into cornstarch; stir in sugar and ½ cup cold *water*. Set aside. Heat wok over high heat; add oil. Stir-fry gingerroot 30 seconds. Add carrots and onion; stir-fry 5 minutes. Remove from wok. Add cauliflower and peas to wok; stir-fry 5 minutes. Stir soy mixture; stir into wok. Cook and stir till thickened and bubbly. Cook and stir 2 minutes more. Stir in tofu, walnuts, carrots, and onion. Cover and cook about 3 minutes or till heated through. Serve over rice. Makes 3 servings.

MEATLESS DISHES

Spicy Pea and Potato Stew

1 cup dry split peas
1 medium onion, chopped
1 stalk celery, chopped
1 clove garlic, minced
½ teaspoon ground cumin
½ teaspoon ground ginger
¼ teaspoon ground turmeric
¼ teaspoon ground red pepper
3 medium potatoes
2 cups coarsely chopped cabbage
1 cup plain yogurt
1 cup chopped peanuts

Rinse split peas. In wok combine peas, onion, celery, garlic, cumin, ginger, turmeric, and red pepper. Add 3 cups *water* and ½ teaspoon *salt*. Bring mixture to boiling; reduce heat. Cover and simmer for 30 minutes.

Peel and cube potatoes; stir into wok. Stir in cabbage. Cover and simmer about 15 minutes more or till peas and potatoes are done. Gradually stir about *1 cup* of the hot mixture into yogurt; return to wok. Stir in peanuts. Heat through, *but do not boil*. Makes 6 servings.

Tofu-Cheese Supper

2 tablespoons butter *or* margarine
1 medium onion, sliced
1 medium carrot, chopped
3 slices white *or* whole wheat bread, torn
6 ounces tofu (bean curd)
6 ounces *process* Swiss cheese
3 eggs
1½ cups milk
½ teaspoon salt
Dash pepper
Dash ground nutmeg

In wok melt butter or margarine over medium-high heat. Stir-fry onion and carrot about 5 minutes or till onion is very tender. In an 8x8x2-inch baking pan layer torn bread. Spoon onion-carrot mixture atop.

Cut up tofu and cheese. In blender container combine tofu, cheese, eggs, milk, salt, pepper, and nutmeg. Cover and blend till smooth. Pour mixture over bread and vegetables; cover with foil.

Wipe out wok; pour boiling water into wok to reach ½ inch below steamer rack. Place pan on rack; cover wok and steam 30 to 35 minutes or till set. Makes 6 servings.

Confetti Macaroni and Cheese

6 ounces elbow macaroni
¼ cup butter *or* margarine
2 medium carrots, chopped
1 stalk celery, chopped
¼ cup all-purpose flour
1 teaspoon salt
¼ teaspoon pepper
¼ teaspoon dried dillweed
2 cups milk
1½ cups cream-style cottage cheese
1 cup frozen peas
1 cup shredded cheddar cheese

Cook macaroni according to package directions; drain and set aside. In wok melt butter or margarine over medium-high heat. Add carrots and celery; stir-fry 5 to 7 minutes or till tender. Stir in flour, salt, pepper, and dillweed. Add milk all at once; cook and stir till thickened and bubbly. Cook and stir 1 minute longer. Stir in cooked macaroni, cottage cheese, and peas. Cook and stir till heated through. Top with cheddar cheese. Makes 6 servings.

Vegetable Chili

- **2 tablespoons cooking oil**
- **1 medium onion, chopped**
- **1 stalk celery, sliced**
- **1 medium zucchini or yellow summer squash, sliced**
- **1½ teaspoons chili powder**
- **1 teaspoon Worcestershire sauce**
- **¼ teaspoon ground red pepper**
- **1 15-ounce can red kidney beans**
- **1 8-ounce can whole kernel corn**
- **1 8-ounce can tomato sauce**
- **1 cup tomato juice**
- **½ cup sliced pitted ripe olives**
- **1 cup shredded cheddar or Monterey Jack cheese**

Heat wok over high heat; add oil. Stir-fry onion, celery, and zucchini for 5 minutes. Stir in chili powder, Worcestershire sauce, and red pepper; stir-fry 1 minute. Stir in *undrained* beans, *undrained* corn, tomato sauce, tomato juice, and olives. Bring to boiling; reduce heat. Simmer, uncovered, about 10 minutes or till slightly thickened. Pass shredded cheese to sprinkle atop chili. Makes 4 servings.

Cheese-Stuffed Eggplant

- **1 eggplant, halved lengthwise (1½ pounds)**
- **2 tablespoons butter or margarine**
- **1 medium onion, chopped**
- **1 cup chopped fresh mushrooms**
- **2 cups cooked rice**
- **1½ cups shredded Swiss or cheddar cheese**
- **¼ cup chopped cashews or almonds**

Scoop out eggplant pulp, leaving two ½-inch-thick shells. Chop eggplant pulp. In wok melt butter over medium-high heat. Stir-fry onion and mushrooms 1 minute. Add chopped eggplant pulp; stir-fry 3 minutes or till tender. Stir in rice, *1 cup* of the cheese, and the nuts; spoon into eggplant shells. Cover loosely with foil.

Wipe out wok. Pour boiling water into wok to reach ½ inch below steamer rack. Place eggplant shells on rack. Cover wok; steam 15 to 20 minutes or till eggplant is done. Remove foil; top eggplant with remaining cheese. Cover wok; steam 2 minutes. Makes 4 servings.

Summer Vegetable Scramble

- **2 tablespoons butter or margarine**
- **1 clove garlic, minced**
- **1 zucchini or yellow summer squash, chopped**
- **2 green onions, sliced**
- **6 beaten eggs**
- **¼ cup milk**
- **½ teaspoon dried basil, crushed**

In wok melt butter or margarine over medium-high heat. Stir-fry garlic 30 seconds. Add zucchini and onions; stir-fry 3 to 5 minutes or till tender. Reduce heat to medium-low. Beat together eggs, milk, basil, ¼ teaspoon *salt,* and ⅛ teaspoon *pepper;* pour over vegetables. Cook without stirring till mixture starts to set on bottom; lift and fold over with spatula so uncooked portion goes to bottom. Continue lifting and folding 5 to 8 minutes or till eggs are done. Garnish with tomato wedges and snipped parsley, if desired. Makes 3 servings.

MEATLESS DISHES

Garnishes

It's fun and easy to dress up your food with garnishes. Use your imagination and a recipe ingredient (or a complementary food) to make a dish as appealing to the eye as it is to the taste. Here are some simple ideas.

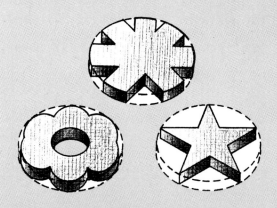

Make colorful cutouts from sturdy vegetables. Thinly slice carrots, rutabagas, and beets, then cut the slices with hors d'oeuvre cutters into fancy shapes. Or, use a sharp knife to design your own stars, flowers, or even letters and numbers. Arrange groups of these atop food as you like.

Carve a simple design in a mushroom cap to garnish Egg Foo Yung or another favorite recipe. Simply cut shallow wedges in the cap with a small sharp knife, saving the cutouts and stems to use in the recipe. Set the carved mushroom caps on a bed of parsley or shredded lettuce, if desired.

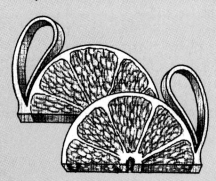

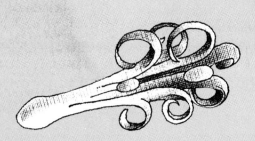

Make lemon or lime slices extra special with an easy twist of the peel. Slice the fruit crosswise, then halve each slice. To loosen peel from fruit, cut around slice through white membrane to within ¼ inch of opposite end. Tuck loosened peel under to form a loop. These are also pretty in water glasses or iced tea. Another time, use orange or grapefruit slices.

Green onion brushes are among the simplest yet most beautiful of garnishes. To make them, trim ¼ inch from tops and bottoms of green onions. At one or both ends, cut several lengthwise slashes about 2 inches long. Cover cut onions with ice water so the cut ends will curl. Drain well and place alongside food. Use the same technique to make celery brushes.

Even if you don't have the time or inclination to do anything fancy with a food, remember the traditional garnishes that can set off a meal: parsley sprigs, olive slices, red or green pepper slices, hard-cooked egg slices, cherry tomatoes, spiced apple rings, and radishes.

Egg Foo Yung

1 cup chicken broth *or*
   vegetable broth
½ cup sliced fresh mushrooms
2 tablespoons soy sauce
1 tablespoon cornstarch
1 teaspoon sugar
2 tablespoons cooking oil
1 stalk celery, thinly bias sliced
   (¾ cup)
¼ cup sliced green onion
1 cup fresh bean sprouts
1 small green pepper, chopped
6 beaten eggs
¼ teaspoon salt
¼ teaspoon pepper

In saucepan combine broth and mushrooms; simmer 5 minutes. Mix soy sauce, cornstarch, and sugar; add to simmering broth. Cook and stir till thickened and bubbly; cook and stir 2 minutes more. Cover and keep warm.

Heat wok over high heat; add oil. Stir-fry celery and onion 1 minute. Add bean sprouts and green pepper; stir-fry 2 to 3 minutes or till just crisp-tender. Reduce heat to medium. Combine eggs, salt, and pepper; pour into wok. Cook without stirring 2 minutes or till eggs begin to set around edges. Lift edges so uncooked portion flows underneath. Continue cooking and lifting till eggs are almost done. Carefully slip entire mixture onto a plate. Flip over and return to wok, browned side up. Cook 1 to 2 minutes or till eggs are done. Slip onto plate; spoon mushroom mixture over eggs. Makes 3 servings.

Brunch Eggs Florentine

¼ cup butter *or* margarine
1 10-ounce package frozen
   chopped spinach, thawed
   and drained
2 green onions, sliced
2 tablespoons all-purpose flour
½ teaspoon salt
⅛ teaspoon ground nutmeg
1 cup milk
1 cup shredded Swiss *or*
   cheddar cheese (4 ounces)
4 eggs

In wok melt butter or margarine over medium-high heat. Stir-fry spinach and onions for 5 minutes. Stir in flour, salt, and nutmeg. Add milk all at once; cook and stir till thickened and bubbly. Cook and stir 1 minute more. Stir in *half* the cheese till melted. Divide mixture among four 8-ounce ramekins or custard cups, making an indentation in center of each. Carefully slide one egg into each indentation. Sprinkle each egg with *2 tablespoons* of the remaining cheese. Cover each loosely with foil.

Wipe out wok; add boiling water to reach ½ inch below steamer rack. Arrange ramekins on rack; cover wok and steam 15 to 20 minutes or till eggs are done. Sprinkle with paprika, if desired. Makes 4 servings.

Eggs Creole

1 16-ounce can tomatoes, cut up
½ cup chopped celery
¼ cup chopped green pepper
¼ cup chopped onion
½ teaspoon salt
⅛ teaspoon pepper
1 bay leaf
1 cup fresh *or* frozen peas
4 eggs
1 cup shredded cheddar cheese

In wok combine *undrained* tomatoes, celery, green pepper, onion, salt, pepper, and bay leaf. Bring to boiling; reduce heat. Cover and simmer about 15 minutes or till vegetables are done. Stir in peas; cook 5 minutes. Remove bay leaf. Break eggs one at a time into a saucer; then slip into simmering tomato mixture, taking care not to break yolks. Sprinkle with salt and pepper. Cover and simmer for 7 to 8 minutes or till eggs are done. Sprinkle with cheese. Cover and cook 1 minute longer or till cheese melts. Pass bottled hot pepper sauce, if desired. Makes 4 servings.

CREATIVE LEFTOVERS

Fried Rice Plus

- **1 egg**
- **2 tablespoons soy sauce**
- **⅛ teaspoon pepper**
- **3 tablespoons cooking oil**
- **1 clove garlic, minced**
- **1 teaspoon grated gingerroot** *or*
  - **¼ teaspoon ground ginger**
- **3 cups** *cold* **cooked rice**
- **4 green onions, sliced**
- **2 cups cubed cooked meat***
- **1½ cups chopped cooked vegetable** or **one 8-ounce can peas, drained**
- **¼ cup chopped peanuts**

In small bowl beat egg with fork; stir in soy sauce and pepper. Set aside. Heat wok over high heat; add oil. Stir-fry garlic and ginger in hot oil 30 seconds. Add rice and onions; stir-fry 5 minutes. Stir in cooked meat, vegetable, and nuts. Cook, stirring often, for 6 to 8 minutes. Drizzle egg mixture over rice mixture, stirring constantly about 1 minute or till egg is set. Pass additional soy sauce, if desired. Makes 4 servings.

   ***Meat suggestions:** chicken, pork, beef, shrimp.

   ****Vegetable suggestions:** carrots, broccoli, turnips, green beans, asparagus.

Curry Plus

- **2 tablespoons butter** *or* **margarine**
- **1 medium onion, chopped**
- **1 clove garlic, minced**
- **1 tablespoon curry powder**
- **¼ cup all-purpose flour**
- **½ teaspoon salt**
- **3 cups cubed cooked meat***
- **1 cup plain yogurt**
- **1 cup chicken broth**
- **1 cup chopped mixed dried fruits**
- **⅓ cup chopped walnuts, pecans,** *or* **peanuts**
- **Hot cooked rice**

In wok melt butter or margarine over medium-high heat. Stir-fry onion, garlic, and curry powder 5 minutes. Stir in flour and salt (omit salt if using ham). Add meat, yogurt, and chicken broth. Cook and stir till thickened and bubbly; cook and stir 1 minute longer. Stir in dried fruits and nuts; heat through. Season to taste. Serve over hot cooked rice. Makes 4 to 6 servings.

   ***Meat suggestions:** lamb, turkey, beef, ham, chicken.

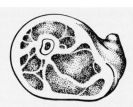

Jambalaya Plus

2 slices bacon, cut up
1 large onion, chopped
1 large green pepper, chopped
2 cloves garlic, minced
⅔ cup long grain rice
2 cups cubed cooked meat*
1 16-ounce can tomatoes, cut up
1 cup dry white wine *or* chicken broth
1 bay leaf
½ teaspoon salt
¼ teaspoon bottled hot pepper sauce
1 cup cooked vegetable**

In wok cook bacon over medium-high heat for 2 minutes. Add onion, green pepper, and garlic; stir-fry 5 minutes. Stir in uncooked rice; stir-fry 1 minute. Add meat. Stir in *undrained* tomatoes, wine or broth, bay leaf, salt, and hot pepper sauce. Reduce heat; cover and simmer for 15 to 20 minutes or till rice is nearly done. Cut cooked vegetable into ½-inch pieces, if necessary. Stir vegetable into wok; cover and simmer 5 minutes longer. Makes 4 to 6 servings.

*Meat suggestions: chicken, ham, fish, beef, pork.

**Vegetable suggestions: okra, green beans, peas, corn, lima beans.

Chili Mac Plus

2 tablespoons cooking oil
1 large onion, chopped
1 large green pepper, chopped
1 16-ounce can tomatoes, cut up
1 15-ounce can red kidney beans
1 8-ounce can tomato sauce
1 4-ounce can green chili peppers, rinsed, seeded, and chopped
2 teaspoons chili powder
1 teaspoon salt
2 cups chopped cooked meat*
2 cups elbow macaroni
  Shredded cheddar cheese

Heat wok over high heat; add oil. Stir-fry onion and green pepper in oil about 5 minutes or till onion is tender but not brown. Stir in *undrained* tomatoes, *undrained* beans, tomato sauce, chili peppers, chili powder, salt, and ½ cup *water*. Bring to boiling; stir in meat and uncooked macaroni. Reduce heat; cover and simmer for 15 to 20 minutes or till macaroni is done. Garnish each serving with cheese. Makes 6 servings.

*Meat suggestions: frankfurters, beef, pork, ham, chicken.

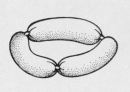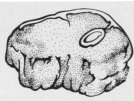

CREATIVE LEFTOVERS

Spaghetti Plus

- **1 tablespoon cooking oil**
- **1 medium onion, chopped**
- **1 stalk celery, chopped**
- **1 clove garlic, minced**
- **1 28-ounce can tomatoes, finely chopped**
- **1 8-ounce can tomato sauce**
- **2 tablespoons snipped parsley**
- **1 bay leaf**
- **1 teaspoon dried basil, crushed**
- **½ teaspoon salt**
- **½ teaspoon dried oregano, crushed**
- **2 cups chopped cooked meat***
- **1 cup cooked vegetable, cut into ½-inch pieces****
- **Hot cooked spaghetti**

Heat wok over high heat; add oil. Stir-fry onion, celery, and garlic for 5 minutes. Stir in *undrained* tomatoes, tomato sauce, parsley, bay leaf, basil, salt, oregano, and ⅛ teaspoon *pepper.* Bring to boiling; reduce heat. Simmer, uncovered, for 25 minutes. Stir in meat and vegetable; heat through. Remove bay leaf. Serve over hot cooked spaghetti. Makes 4 to 6 servings.

  * Meat suggestions: beef, pork, turkey, ham, liver.

  **Vegetable suggestions: carrots, asparagus, green beans, zucchini, cauliflower.

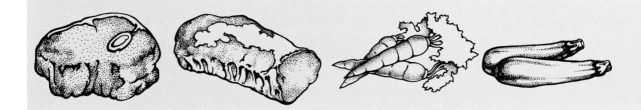

Carbonara Plus

- **4 slices bacon, cut up**
- **4 cups sliced fresh mushrooms**
- **2 cups cubed cooked meat***
- **10 ounces spaghetti *or* linguine, cooked and drained**
- **2 beaten eggs (at room temperature)**
- **¾ cup whipping cream (at room temperature)**
- **½ cup grated Parmesan cheese**

In wok cook bacon over medium-high heat for 5 minutes. Add mushrooms; stir-fry for 5 minutes. Add meat; stir-fry 2 minutes. Add pasta to wok; toss to mix and heat through. Turn off heat. Beat eggs, cream, and Parmesan cheese; pour over mixture in wok. Toss to mix. Serve at once. Makes 6 servings.

  *Meat suggestions: chicken, turkey, beef, ham, pork.

Tetrazzini Plus

⅓ cup butter *or* margarine
1½ cups sliced fresh mushrooms *or* one 6-ounce can sliced mushrooms, drained
⅓ cup all-purpose flour
¼ teaspoon salt
Dash pepper
1 cup chicken broth
1 cup light cream *or* milk
¼ cup grated Parmesan cheese
¼ cup dry sherry
2 cups cubed cooked meat*
2 tablespoons chopped pitted ripe olives
2 tablespoons snipped parsley
Hot cooked spaghetti *or* medium noodles

In wok melt butter or margarine over medium heat. Add mushrooms; stir-fry 3 minutes. Stir in flour, salt, and pepper. Add broth and cream; cook and stir till thickened and bubbly. Cook and stir 1 minute longer. Stir in cheese and sherry. Stir in meat, olives, and parsley; heat through. Serve over spaghetti or noodles. Makes 6 servings.

*Meat suggestions: chicken, turkey, ham, pork, beef.

   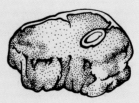

Cheesy Meat and Vegetables Plus

2 tablespoons butter *or* margarine
2 tablespoons all-purpose flour
¼ teaspoon ground nutmeg
1⅓ cups milk
1 cup cooked vegetable*
1 cup cubed cooked meat**
1 3-ounce package cream cheese, cut into cubes
4 English muffins, split and toasted, *or* 4 baked patty shells

In wok melt butter or margarine over medium heat; stir in flour and nutmeg. Add milk all at once; cook and stir till thickened and bubbly. Cook and stir 1 minute longer. Cut vegetable into ½-inch pieces, if necessary. Stir vegetable, meat, and cream cheese into wok. Cook and stir till cheese melts and mixture is heated through. Spoon over English muffins or patty shells; sprinkle with additional nutmeg, if desired. Makes 4 servings.

* Vegetable suggestions: peas, carrots, corn, spinach, green beans.

**Meat suggestions: ham, chicken, turkey, fish, beef.

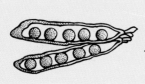  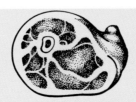 

CREATIVE LEFTOVERS

Barbecue Sandwiches Plus

- 2 **tablespoons cooking oil**
- 1 **medium onion, chopped**
- 1 **stalk celery, chopped**
- 1 **clove garlic, minced**
- 1 **cup chili sauce**
- ½ **cup water**
- 2 **tablespoons brown sugar**
- 2 **tablespoons vinegar**
- 2 **tablespoons Worcestershire sauce**
- 1 **tablespoon soy sauce**
- 1 **pound sliced** *or* **chopped cooked meat* (3 cups)**
- 8 **individual French rolls** *or* **large hamburger buns, split and toasted**

Heat wok over high heat; add oil. Stir-fry onion, celery, and garlic in hot oil for 5 minutes; stir in chili sauce, water, brown sugar, vinegar, Worcestershire sauce, and soy sauce. Bring to boiling; reduce heat. Cover and simmer 10 to 15 minutes. Stir in meat; cook over low heat about 10 minutes, stirring occasionally. Serve on rolls or buns. Makes 8 servings.

*Meat suggestions: pork, beef, turkey, chicken, ham.

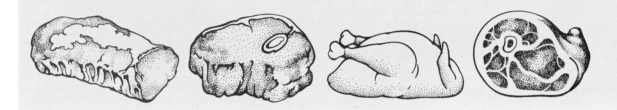

Pizza Sandwiches Plus

- 1 **beaten egg**
- 1 **8-** *or* **10-ounce can pizza sauce**
- ¾ **cup soft bread crumbs**
- ¼ **teaspoon salt**
- ¼ **teaspoon dried oregano, crushed**
- **Dash pepper**
- 1½ **cups ground cooked meat***
- ¼ **cup all-purpose flour**
- **Cooking oil for deep-fat frying**
- 2 **slices mozzarella cheese, halved**
- 4 **hamburger buns, toasted**

In bowl combine egg, *1 tablespoon* of the pizza sauce, bread crumbs, salt, oregano, and pepper (omit salt if using ham). Add meat; mix well. Shape mixture into four ¼-inch-thick patties. Coat patties with flour.

In wok heat 1 to 1½ inches cooking oil to 360°. Fry 2 patties at a time for 3 to 4 minutes or till brown on both sides. Drain on paper toweling. Top each patty with a half slice of cheese; broil 1 to 2 minutes to melt cheese, if desired. Serve on buns with remaining pizza sauce. Makes 4 servings.

*Meat suggestions: chicken, beef, ham, pork, turkey.

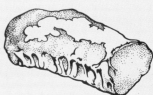

Chimichangas Plus

1 tablespoon cooking oil
2 cloves garlic, minced
2 cups finely chopped cooked
  meat*
1 tomato, peeled and chopped
1 4-ounce can green chili
  peppers, rinsed, seeded,
  and chopped
1 teaspoon dried oregano,
  crushed
½ teaspoon salt
¼ teaspoon ground cumin
  Dash pepper
6 10-inch flour tortillas
  Cooking oil for deep-fat frying

Heat wok over high heat; add 1 tablespoon oil. Stir-fry garlic 30 seconds. Add meat, tomato, chili peppers, oregano, salt, cumin, and pepper (omit salt if using ham); stir-fry 3 minutes longer. Remove from heat. Cool slightly. Spoon about ⅓ cup meat mixture near edge of *each* tortilla. Roll up starting with edge near filling. Push ends of roll to inside tortilla roll to seal in filling and prevent unrolling.

Wash wok. In wok heat 2 inches oil to 365°. Fry 2 or 3 tortilla rolls at a time for 1 to 2 minutes on each side or till golden. Drain on paper toweling. Keep warm in 300° oven while frying remaining tortilla rolls. If desired, serve with guacamole and dairy sour cream. Makes 6 servings.

*Meat suggestions: beef, ham, pork, chicken, turkey.

  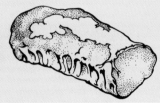 

Uptown Hash Plus

2 tablespoons cooking oil
2 cups cubed cooked potatoes
¼ cup chopped onion
2 cups cubed cooked meat*
⅓ cup dry white wine
3 tablespoons water
½ teaspoon dried basil, crushed
2 tablespoons snipped parsley
2 tablespoons slivered almonds,
  toasted

Heat wok over medium-high heat; add oil. Add potatoes and onion; stir-fry for 3 to 5 minutes or till lightly browned. Stir in meat, wine, water, and basil. Stir-fry 3 minutes more or till liquid is nearly evaporated. Season to taste. Sprinkle with parsley and almonds. Makes 4 servings.

*Meat suggestions: chicken, beef, pork, ham, corned beef, turkey.

  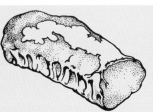 

CREATIVE LEFTOVERS

Taco Salad Plus

1 tablespoon cooking oil
1 small onion, chopped
1 15-ounce can refried beans
½ cup water
⅓ cup taco sauce
½ teaspoon salt
⅛ teaspoon pepper
2 cups chopped cooked meat*
1 8-ounce can whole kernel
    corn, drained
1 medium head lettuce, torn
¼ cup sliced radishes
1 cup shredded Monterey Jack
    or cheddar cheese
1 medium avocado, seeded,
    peeled, and sliced
1 cup corn chips

Heat wok over high heat; add oil. Stir-fry onion till tender but not brown. Stir in refried beans, water, taco sauce, salt, and pepper. Stir in meat and corn. Reduce heat; cover and simmer for 5 minutes.

Divide lettuce among 6 salad bowls; sprinkle with radishes and shredded cheese. Spoon meat mixture over lettuce. Top with avocado slices and corn chips. Serve at once. Makes 6 servings.

*Meat suggestions: beef, pork, chicken, turkey, lamb.

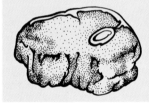

Meaty Eggplant Plus

1 medium eggplant (1 pound)
2 tablespoons cooking oil
1 medium onion, chopped
1 16-ounce can tomatoes, cut up
½ teaspoon garlic salt
½ teaspoon salt
½ teaspoon dried thyme,
    crushed
¼ teaspoon ground cinnamon
3 cups chopped cooked meat*
2 tablespoons cold water
1 tablespoon all-purpose flour
1 cup shredded Swiss cheese

Peel and cube eggplant. Heat wok over high heat; add oil. Stir-fry eggplant and onion in hot oil for 5 minutes; stir in *undrained* tomatoes, garlic salt, salt, thyme, and cinnamon. Stir in meat; bring to boiling. Reduce heat; cover and simmer 10 minutes or till eggplant is done, stirring occasionally. Stir water into flour; stir into wok. Cook and stir till thickened and bubbly; cook and stir 1 minute longer. Top with cheese; cover and cook 1 to 2 minutes more or till cheese melts. Makes 8 servings.

*Meat suggestions: lamb, beef, pork, chicken, turkey.

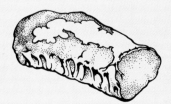

Stuffed Romaine Rolls Plus

1 beaten egg
2 tablespoons milk
½ cup finely chopped cooked vegetable*
1 tablespoon horseradish mustard
2 cups ground cooked meat**
¾ cup cooked rice
12 large romaine leaves
2 tablespoons butter
2 tablespoons all-purpose flour
2 tablespoons horseradish mustard
1 teaspoon instant chicken bouillon granules
1 cup milk
Paprika

In bowl combine egg, 2 tablespoons milk, cooked vegetable, and 1 tablespoon mustard. Add meat and rice; mix well. Trim thin slices from heavy center rib of each romaine leaf so it lies flat, keeping leaf in one piece. Immerse leaves in boiling water 1 to 2 minutes or till limp; drain. Place 2 leaves together, overlapping one long edge slightly; at one end, place scant ½ cup meat mixture. Fold in sides; roll up, making sure folded sides are included in roll. Repeat.

Pour boiling water into wok to reach ½ inch below steamer rack. Arrange romaine rolls on heatproof plate; place on rack. Cover wok and steam about 25 minutes.

Meanwhile, for sauce, in saucepan melt butter; stir in flour, 2 tablespoons mustard, and bouillon. Add 1 cup milk; cook and stir till thickened and bubbly. Cook and stir 1 minute longer. Spoon over rolls; sprinkle with paprika. Serves 6.

* Vegetable suggestions: carrots, broccoli, potatoes.
**Meat suggestions: ham, corned beef, beef, pork, lamb.

Steamed Timbales Plus

1½ cups milk
1 cup shredded American cheese (4 ounces)
3 beaten eggs
1½ cups soft bread crumbs
¼ cup chopped onion
¼ teaspoon salt
¼ teaspoon dry mustard
1½ cups finely chopped cooked meat*
1 cup finely chopped cooked vegetable** *or* cooked peas

In saucepan combine milk and cheese; heat and stir over low heat till cheese melts. Cool slightly; gradually stir into eggs. Stir in crumbs, onion, salt, and mustard. Toss meat and vegetable together; divide among four 10-ounce custard cups or ramekins. Pour egg mixture into each; cover each cup with foil.

Pour boiling water into wok to reach ½ inch below steamer rack; arrange cups on rack. Cover wok and steam 25 to 30 minutes or till knife inserted off center comes out clean. Let stand 5 minutes. Makes 4 servings.

* Meat suggestions: chicken, veal, fish, lamb, beef.
**Vegetable suggestions: broccoli, spinach.

SIDE DISHES

Of course, vegetables of all kinds respond well to stir-frying, steaming, and deep-fat frying in a wok; but this chapter allows you to expand your usual side dishes to include rice, pasta, breads, even salads. Easy-to-read charts give directions for steaming and stir-frying most of the popular vegetables.

Lentil Pilaf (see recipe, page 69)

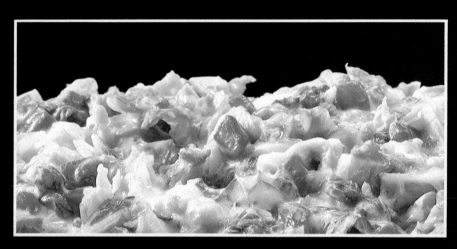

Creamed Chinese Cabbage (see recipe, page 65)

Bacon-Fried Carrots and Turnips (see recipe, page 66)

Pictured below: Hush Puppies (see recipe, page 70)

SIDE DISHES

Steamed Vegetables

Prepare fresh vegetable as directed in the chart below. Pour boiling water into wok to reach about ½ inch below steamer rack. Arrange vegetables on steamer rack in wok; avoid overcrowding so steam can circulate evenly around vegetables. Cover wok and steam for the amount of time specified in the chart. When vegetable is done, remove to serving dish and season to taste with salt, pepper, and butter or margarine. For more information on steaming in a wok, see page 13.

Vegetable	Quantity	Preparation Directions	Cooking Time
asparagus	1 pound	remove tough portion of stem	10 to 12 minutes
broccoli	1 pound	cut into spears	10 to 15 minutes
cabbage	½ medium head	core and cut into wedges	15 to 20 minutes
carrots	6 medium (3 cups)	slice	10 to 15 minutes
cauliflower	1 medium head 1 medium head	whole; remove leaves and stem break into flowerets	20 to 25 minutes 10 to 15 minutes
corn on cob	4 ears	remove husk and silk	8 to 10 minutes
green beans	1 pound	whole; remove ends	15 to 20 minutes
okra	1 pound 1 pound	whole; cut off stems slice	10 to 15 minutes 8 to 10 minutes
pea pods	6 to 8 ounces (3 cups)	whole; remove blossoms and stems	3 to 5 minutes
potatoes (new)	2 pounds	choose small potatoes; peel strip around center	20 to 25 minutes
spinach	1 pound	remove stems; tear leaves	4 to 5 minutes
squash (winter)	1 pound	cut into pieces and remove seeds before cooking; peel after cooking	15 to 20 minutes
zucchini or yellow summer squash	1 pound (3½ cups)	slice ¼ inch thick	5 to 10 minutes

Stir-Fried Vegetables

Prepare fresh vegetable as directed in the chart below; cook no more than the specified quantity for best results. (If desired, you can mix different vegetables with similar cooking times.) Heat wok over high heat; add 2 tablespoons *cooking oil*.

When oil is hot, add prepared vegetable. Stir-fry over high heat for the time specified in the chart or till vegetable is crisp-tender. Season with soy sauce, lemon juice, salt, and pepper, if desired. For more information on stir-frying, see page 10.

Vegetable	Quantity	Preparation Directions	Cooking Time
asparagus	1 pound	remove tough portion of stem; bias-slice into 1-inch pieces	5 minutes
bok choy	1 small bunch (4 cups)	thinly slice	3 minutes
broccoli	1 pound	cut buds into bite-size pieces; thinly slice stems	5 to 6 minutes
cabbage	½ medium head (3 cups)	core and coarsely shred or chop	3 minutes
carrots	6 medium (3 cups)	very thinly slice	5 to 6 minutes
cauliflower	½ medium head (3 cups)	remove leaves and stem; slice	5 minutes
celery	4 stalks (2 cups)	thinly slice	5 to 7 minutes
green beans	1 pound	bias-slice into 1-inch pieces	5 to 7 minutes
mushrooms	1 pound	slice	2 to 3 minutes
pea pods	6 to 8 ounces (3 cups)	whole; remove blossoms and stems	2 to 3 minutes
spinach	1 pound	remove stems; tear leaves	2 to 3 minutes
zucchini or yellow summer squash	1 pound (3½ cups)	slice	3 to 4 minutes

SIDE DISHES

Spinach in Sour Cream Sauce

2 tablespoons butter *or* margarine
¼ cup sliced green onion
6 cups torn fresh spinach *or* turnip greens
1 cup sliced fresh mushrooms
1 tablespoon all-purpose flour
½ cup dairy sour cream
¼ cup milk
Dash ground nutmeg

In wok melt butter or margarine over medium-high heat, Add green onion; stir-fry 2 minutes. Add spinach or turnip greens and mushrooms. Reduce heat; cover and cook over low heat for 4 minutes. Stir flour into sour cream; stir in milk. Add sour cream mixture to wok; cook and stir till thickened and bubbly. Cook and stir 1 minute longer. Season to taste with salt, pepper, and ground nutmeg. Makes 4 servings.

Herbed Zucchini Spears

½ cup all-purpose flour
1 teaspoon seasoned salt
½ teaspoon onion salt
½ teaspoon Italian seasoning
¼ teaspoon seasoned pepper
1 slightly beaten egg
¼ cup milk
1 tablespoon cooking oil
Cooking oil for deep-fat frying
3 medium zucchini, cut into ½-inch julienne strips

In bowl stir together flour, seasoned salt, onion salt, Italian seasoning, and seasoned pepper. Combine egg, milk, and 1 tablespoon oil; gradually add to flour mixture, beating till smooth.

In wok heat 1½ inches cooking oil to 360°. Dip zucchini pieces into flour mixture; fry several at a time in hot oil for 4 to 5 minutes or till golden. Drain on paper toweling; serve at once. Makes 6 servings.

Creole Mixed Vegetables

2 tablespoons cooking oil
1 large green pepper, chopped
1 medium onion, chopped
1 10-ounce package frozen cut okra
1 10-ounce package frozen whole kernel corn
1 7½-ounce can tomatoes, cut up
½ teaspoon salt
½ teaspoon dried thyme, crushed
Few dashes bottled hot pepper sauce
Hot cooked rice

Heat wok over high heat; add oil. Stir-fry green pepper and onion for 5 minutes. Stir in okra, corn, *undrained* tomatoes, salt, thyme, and pepper sauce. Cover and cook over medium-high heat for 5 minutes or till vegetables are done and liquid is slightly thickened. Serve with rice and additional hot pepper sauce, if desired. Makes 6 to 8 servings.

SIDE DISHES

Wilted Spinach Salad

- 8 cups fresh spinach
- 1 cup fresh bean sprouts
- ½ cup sliced water chestnuts
- 4 slices bacon, cut into small pieces
- ¼ cup finely chopped onion
- 3 tablespoons vinegar
- 3 tablespoons catsup
- 1 tablespoon sugar

Tear spinach leaves into bite-size pieces; place in mixing bowl. Add bean sprouts and water chestnuts. In wok cook bacon pieces over medium heat till crisp; do not drain. Add onion, vinegar, catsup, and sugar to wok. Cook and stir till mixture is bubbly and heated through. Remove from heat. Add spinach mixture to wok, tossing till greens are slightly wilted and well coated. Turn into serving bowl; serve at once. Garnish with sliced hard-cooked egg, if desired. Makes 8 servings.

Celery with Almonds

- 1 tablespoon cornstarch
- ½ teaspoon salt
- ⅛ teapoon pepper
- ½ cup light cream *or* milk
- 2 tablespoons butter *or* margarine
- 3 cups bias-sliced celery
- 1 cup sliced fresh mushrooms
- ¼ cup dry white wine *or* chicken broth
- ¼ cup sliced almonds, toasted

Combine cornstarch, salt, and pepper; stir in cream or milk. Set aside.

In wok melt butter or margarine over medium heat. Add celery and mushrooms; stir-fry for 8 to 10 minutes or till celery is crisp-tender. Stir cream mixture; stir into wok. Cook and stir till thickened and bubbly; cook and stir 2 minutes longer. Stir in wine or broth. Cover and cook 1 minute longer. Garnish with almonds. Makes 4 to 6 servings.

Tarragon Vegetable Medley

- 2 tablespoons cooking oil
- 2 cups cauliflower flowerets
- 1 medium carrot, cut into julienne strips
- 1 medium onion, cut into thin wedges
- 1 medium green pepper, cut into 1-inch squares
- 2 tablespoons white wine vinegar
- 1 tablespoon sugar
- 1 tablespoon water
- ½ teaspoon dried tarragon, crushed
- ¼ teaspoon salt
- ¼ teaspoon sesame *or* walnut oil*
- ⅓ cup pitted ripe olives
  Walnut halves

Heat wok over medium heat; add cooking oil. Stir in cauliflower, carrot, onion, and green pepper to coat well. Cover and cook 7 to 8 minutes or till vegetables are crisp-tender.

Meanwhile, stir together vinegar, sugar, water, tarragon, salt, and sesame or walnut oil. Halve olives; add to wok. Drizzle vinegar mixture over vegetables. Stir-fry about 1 minute longer. Garnish with walnuts; serve hot or cold. Makes 4 servings.

Recipe note: Sesame and walnut oils are highly flavored seasonings used in small amounts. You will find them at food specialty shops and large supermarkets.

Hot Potato Salad

6 **medium potatoes, peeled and
    cubed**
3 **slices bacon, cut up**
1 **medium onion, chopped**
2 **tablespoons all-purpose flour**
¼ **cup sugar**
1 **teaspoon salt**
½ **teaspoon celery seed**
    Dash pepper
⅔ **cup water**
⅓ **cup vinegar**
2 **tablespoons snipped parsley**

In covered wok cook potatoes in small amount of boiling water 15 to 20 minutes or till tender. Drain; set potatoes aside.

In same wok cook bacon over medium-high heat till bacon is crisp. Remove bacon. Drain, reserving 3 tablespoons drippings in wok. Add onion to wok; stir-fry for 3 minutes. Stir in flour; stir in sugar, salt, celery seed, and pepper. Add water and vinegar. Cook and stir till thickened and bubbly; cook and stir 1 minute longer. Stir in potatoes. Cover and simmer for 5 to 10 minutes or till heated through. Top with reserved bacon and parsley. Makes 6 servings.

Creamed Chinese Cabbage *(pictured on pages 58 and 59)*

2 **tablespoons butter** *or*
    margarine
½ **teaspoon grated gingerroot** *or*
    ⅛ teaspoon ground ginger
6 **cups sliced Chinese cabbage**
1 **tablespoon all-purpose flour**
⅓ **cup milk**
2 **tablespoons chopped pimiento**
1 **teaspoon instant chicken
    bouillon granules**

In wok melt butter or margarine over medium-high heat. Add ginger; stir-fry 30 seconds. Add Chinese cabbage; stir-fry 3 minutes. Stir in flour; add milk, pimiento, and bouillon granules. Cook and stir till thickened and bubbly; cook and stir 1 minute longer. Serve at once in sauce dishes. Makes 4 servings.

Green Beans Paprikash

2 **slices bacon, cut up**
1 **medium onion, chopped**
2 **teaspoons paprika**
½ **teaspoon sugar**
½ **teaspoon salt**
⅛ **teaspoon pepper**
2 **cups fresh green beans, cut
    into 1-inch pieces,** *or* **one 9-
    ounce package frozen cut
    green beans**
2 **medium tomatoes, peeled and
    chopped**

In wok cook bacon over medium-high heat till bacon is crisp; remove bacon from wok, reserving drippings. Drain bacon; set aside.

Stir-fry onion in drippings over medium-high heat till onion is tender; stir in paprika, sugar, salt, and pepper. Add beans; stir-fry 5 to 7 minutes or till nearly crisp-tender. Stir in tomatoes; stir-fry 5 minutes longer. Sprinkle with reserved bacon. Makes 4 servings.

SIDE DISHES

Bacon-Fried Carrots and Turnips (pictured on pages 58 and 59)

2 slices bacon, cut up
3 medium carrots, cut into
    julienne strips
2 turnips, cut into julienne strips
    (2 cups)
1 medium onion, sliced
½ teaspoon salt
⅛ teaspoon pepper

In wok cook bacon over medium-high heat till crisp; remove bacon from wok, reserving drippings. Drain bacon and set aside. Stir-fry carrots, turnips, and onion in drippings about 5 minutes or till carrots are crisp-tender. Sprinkle with salt and pepper. Cover and cook over low heat for 8 to 10 minutes or till vegetables are done. Top with reserved bacon and garnish with snipped parsley, if desired. Makes 6 servings.

Sautéed Cucumbers

4 medium cucumbers *or*
    zucchini
1 tablespoon butter *or*
    margarine
½ teaspoon salt
½ teaspoon dried dillweed
½ cup dairy sour cream
2 teaspoons all-purpose flour

Halve cucumbers or zucchini lengthwise; trim off ends and scoop out seeds. Cut seeded vegetables into ¼-inch slices. In wok melt butter over medium-high heat. Stir-fry cucumbers, salt, and dill for 5 to 7 minutes or till crisp-tender. Stir sour cream and flour together; stir into cucumbers. Cook over low heat about 3 minutes or till heated through; *do not boil.* Makes 6 servings.

Sherried Mushrooms and Peppers

2 small onions
1 small green pepper
2 tablespoons butter *or*
    margarine
8 ounces fresh mushrooms,
    halved (3 cups)
2 tablespoons dry sherry
¾ teaspoon salt

Cut onions into thin wedges; cut green pepper into ½-inch squares. In wok melt butter or margarine over medium-high heat. Add onions; stir-fry for 5 minutes. Add green pepper, mushrooms, sherry, and salt; cook 3 to 5 minutes longer or till peppers are crisp-tender, stirring occasionally. Makes 4 to 6 servings.

Buttery Cabbage and Carrots

3 tablespoons butter *or*
    margarine
1 medium onion, sliced
½ medium head cabbage, cored
    and coarsely chopped
4 medium carrots, shredded
1 teaspoon salt
1 teaspoon celery seed
1 tablespoon lemon juice

In wok melt butter or margarine over medium-high heat. Add onion; stir-fry 2 minutes. Add cabbage, carrots, salt, and celery seed. Cover and cook over medium heat about 10 minutes or till cabbage is crisp-tender, stirring occasionally. Stir in lemon juice. Makes 8 servings.

Curried Vegetables

2 tablespoons cooking oil
2 medium onions, sliced
1 clove garlic, minced
2 teaspoons curry powder
2 medium potatoes, peeled
   and cut into ½-inch cubes
   (2 cups)
4 carrots, bias sliced (2 cups)
1 cup fresh *or* frozen peas
½ cup water
1 teaspoon instant vegetable
   bouillon granules
½ teaspoon salt

Heat wok over high heat; add oil. Stir-fry onions and garlic for 3 minutes. Sprinkle with curry powder; stir-fry 1 minute longer. Stir in potatoes, carrots, peas, water, bouillon granules, and salt. Cover and simmer for 10 to 15 minutes or till vegetables are done. Makes 4 to 6 servings.

Brown Rice and Vegetables

1⅓ cups water
¼ teaspoon salt
½ cup brown rice
1 cup fresh pea pods, halved
   crosswise, *or* one 6-ounce
   package frozen pea pods
1 tablespoon cooking oil
½ cup bias-sliced carrots
4 green onions, bias sliced into
   1-inch lengths
1 small green pepper, cut into
   bite-size pieces
1 small clove garlic, minced
1 cup sliced fresh mushrooms
1 tablespoon soy sauce

In 1-quart saucepan bring water and salt to boiling. Stir in uncooked brown rice. Cover and simmer for 45 to 50 minutes or till tender. If using frozen pea pods, rinse under hot water to separate; drain.

   Heat wok over high heat; add oil. Stir-fry carrots 2 minutes. Add onions, green pepper, and garlic; stir-fry 2 minutes. Add more oil, if needed. Add mushrooms, pea pods, and cooked rice to wok; stir-fry 2 to 3 minutes more. Stir in soy sauce. Makes 4 to 6 servings.

Savory Rice

½ of a lemon
2 tablespoons butter *or*
   margarine
2 cloves garlic, minced
1 cup long grain rice
⅓ cup sliced green onion
¼ teaspoon dried rosemary,
   crushed
2½ cups chicken broth

Using a vegetable peeler, thinly peel the lemon half. Set peel aside; reserve lemon for another use. In wok melt butter or margarine over medium heat. Add lemon peel and garlic; stir-fry 1 minute. Discard lemon peel. Add uncooked rice, onion, and rosemary to wok; stir-fry for 5 minutes. Stir in chicken broth; bring to boiling. Reduce heat; cover and simmer about 20 minutes or till rice is done. Makes 6 servings.

Cheese-Broccoli Rice

¼ cup butter *or* margarine
1 stalk celery, chopped
1 medium green pepper, chopped
2 cups chopped fresh broccoli *or* one 10-ounce package frozen chopped broccoli, thawed and drained
1 cup long grain rice
2¼ cups water
1 11-ounce can condensed cheddar cheese soup
½ teaspoon dried basil, crushed
¼ teaspoon salt

In wok melt butter or margarine over medium-high heat. Add celery and green pepper; stir-fry for 3 minutes. Add broccoli and uncooked rice; stir-fry 3 minutes longer. Stir in water, condensed soup, basil, and salt. Bring to boiling. Reduce heat; cover and simmer about 20 minutes or till rice and broccoli are done, stirring often. Makes 6 servings.

Lentil Pilaf (pictured on pages 58 and 59)

4 slices bacon, cut up
1 medium onion, thinly sliced
1 medium tomato, peeled and chopped
½ cup dry lentils
2¾ cups chicken broth
½ cup long grain rice
½ teaspoon ground sage
⅛ teaspoon ground red pepper
¼ cup snipped parsley

In wok cook bacon over medium heat till crisp; drain, reserving 2 tablespoons drippings in wok. Crumble bacon and set aside. Add onion and tomato to drippings in wok; stir-fry for 5 minutes. Rinse lentils; stir into onion mixture. Stir in chicken broth, uncooked rice, sage, and red pepper. Bring to boiling; reduce heat. Cover and simmer for 30 to 35 minutes or till lentils and rice are tender. Stir in snipped parsley and crumbled bacon. Makes 5 servings.

Twice-Cooked Noodles

6 ounces fine noodles *or* spaghetti
3 tablespoons soy sauce
1 teaspoon cornstarch
⅓ cup cold water
½ teaspoon curry powder
3 tablespoons cooking oil
1 clove garlic, minced
1 medium onion, sliced
½ cup chopped fresh broccoli
1 cup sliced fresh mushrooms
½ cup shredded carrot
1 tablespoon cooking oil
3 cups shredded cabbage

In saucepan cook noodles according to package directions. Rinse in cold water and drain well. Stir soy sauce into cornstarch; stir in water and curry. Set aside.

Heat wok over high heat; add *1 tablespoon* oil. Add *half* the noodles; stir-fry for 7 to 9 minutes or till lightly browned. Remove to plate. Repeat with *1 tablespoon* more oil and the remaining noodles. Add 1 tablespoon oil to wok; stir-fry garlic for 30 seconds. Add onion; stir-fry 2 minutes. Add broccoli; stir-fry 2 minutes. Add mushrooms and carrot; stir-fry 2 minutes. Stir soy sauce mixture; stir into vegetables. Cook and stir till thickened and bubbly; cook and stir 2 minutes more. Stir in noodles; heat through. Remove from wok; keep warm.

Add 1 tablespoon oil to wok; stir-fry cabbage 3 minutes or till crisp-tender. Arrange on platter; top with noodle mixture. Makes 6 to 8 servings.

Twice-Cooked Noodles

SIDE DISHES

Hush Puppies (pictured on pages 58 and 59)

2 cups cornmeal
½ cup all-purpose flour
1 tablespoon sugar
2 teaspoons baking powder
½ teaspoon baking soda
½ teaspoon salt
1 beaten egg
1¼ cups buttermilk *or* sour milk
⅓ cup finely chopped onion *or* green onion
　Cooking oil for deep-fat frying

In mixing bowl combine cornmeal, flour, sugar, baking powder, baking soda, and salt. Combine egg, buttermilk or sour milk, and onion; stir into the cornmeal mixture till moistened.

In wok heat 1½ inches cooking oil to 375°. Drop batter into the hot oil by tablespoonfuls. Fry a few at a time about 2 minutes or till golden brown, turning once. Drain on paper toweling; serve warm. Makes about 24.

Corn Oysters

2 ears corn on the cob *or* one 8-ounce can whole kernel corn, drained
1 beaten egg
¼ cup all-purpose flour
3 tablespoons light cream *or* milk
1 tablespoon butter *or* margarine, melted
¼ teaspoon salt
⅛ teaspoon pepper
　Cooking oil for deep-fat frying

If using fresh corn, remove husks and silks. With sharp knife, cut down through the center of kernels on each row of corn; scrape corn off cob. (If using canned corn, coarsely chop the corn.) In bowl combine egg, flour, cream or milk, butter or margarine, salt, pepper, and corn.

In wok heat 1½ inches cooking oil to 365°. Carefully drop corn mixture into the hot oil by tablespoonfuls. Fry a few at a time about 2 minutes or till golden, turning once. Drain on paper toweling. Makes about 12.

Potato Puffs

1 cup all-purpose flour
2 tablespoons snipped parsley
1½ teaspoons baking powder
½ teaspoon salt
⅛ teaspoon onion powder
2 beaten eggs
1 cup mashed potatoes*
　Cooking oil for deep-fat frying

In mixing bowl combine flour, parsley, baking powder, salt, and onion powder. Stir in beaten eggs and mashed potatoes, mixing well.

In wok heat 1½ inches cooking oil to 365°. Using about 1 rounded tablespoon for each, drop potato mixture into hot oil. Fry a few at a time for 3 to 4 minutes or till golden brown. Drain on paper toweling. Makes about 24.

*Recipe note: This recipe is a wonderful way to use leftover mashed potatoes, but it's also delicious made with quickly prepared instant mashed potatoes. Prepare the potatoes according to package directions; cool before using.

Penuche-Nut Rolls

1 to 1½ cups all-purpose flour
1 package active dry yeast
½ cup milk
3 tablespoons sugar
2 tablespoons shortening
½ teaspoon salt
1 tablespoon butter or
    margarine, melted
¼ cup packed brown sugar
¼ cup chopped walnuts
½ teaspoon ground cinnamon
    Maple-Penuche Glaze

In small mixer bowl combine ½ cup of the flour and the yeast. In saucepan heat together milk, sugar, shortening, and salt just till warm (115° to 120°), stirring till shortening almost melts. Add to dry mixture; beat at low speed of electric mixer 30 seconds, scraping sides of bowl constantly. Beat 3 minutes at high speed. Stir in as much of the remaining flour as you can mix in with a spoon. Turn out onto lightly floured surface. Knead in enough remaining flour to make a moderately stiff dough (6 to 8 minutes total). Place in lightly greased bowl; turn once to grease surface. Cover; let rise in warm place till double (about 1 hour). Punch dough down; turn out onto lightly floured surface. Cover and let rest 10 minutes. Roll dough to a 10x6-inch rectangle. Brush with the melted butter or margarine. Combine brown sugar, walnuts, and cinnamon; sprinkle over dough. Roll up, starting at long side. Cut into 12 rolls. Cover and let rise in warm place till nearly double (about 25 minutes).

Pour boiling water into wok to reach ½ inch below steamer rack. Place rolls on lightly greased steamer rack so rolls do not touch. (If all rolls do not fit, use 2 steamer racks or cook in separate batches.) Cover wok and steam about 20 minutes. Transfer to a wire rack. While warm, drizzle with Maple-Penuche Glaze. Makes 12.

Maple-Penuche Glaze: In small saucepan melt ¼ cup *butter or margarine*; stir in ½ cup packed *brown sugar*. Bring to boiling; cook and stir 1 minute or till slightly thick. Cool 15 minutes. Add 2 tablespoons *milk* and ½ teaspoon *maple flavoring*; beat till smooth. Beat in enough sifted *powdered sugar* (about 1 cup) to make of drizzling consistency.

Boston Brown Bread

½ cup whole wheat flour
¼ cup all-purpose flour
¼ cup cornmeal
½ teaspoon baking powder
¼ teaspoon baking soda
¼ teaspoon salt
1 beaten egg
¼ cup light molasses
2 tablespoons sugar
2 teaspoons cooking oil
¾ cup buttermilk or sour milk
¼ cup raisins

Stir together flours, cornmeal, baking powder, soda, and salt. In mixing bowl combine egg, molasses, sugar, and cooking oil. Add flour mixture to molasses mixture alternately with buttermilk; beat well. Stir in raisins. Turn batter into 2 well-greased 16-ounce vegetable cans. Cover each can tightly with foil.

Pour boiling water into wok to reach ½ inch below steamer rack. Place cans on rack; cover wok and steam for 2½ to 3 hours or till bread tests done. Remove cans to a wire rack; cool 10 minutes. Remove bread from cans with spatula. Serve warm. Makes 2 loaves.

Steamed Cakes with Fruit Sauce (see recipe, page 74)

Maple Gingerbread (see recipe, page 79)

Pictured below: Spicy Dried Fruit Compote (see recipe, page 75)

DESSERTS

Desserts made in a wok? You bet! From refreshing fruit desserts to delicate steamed cakes and rich steamed puddings, the wok can provide a dessert for any occasion, even a spectacular flaming finale to a meal.

DESSERTS

Steamed Cakes with Fruit Sauce (pictured on pages 72 and 73)

⅓ cup butter *or* margarine,
    softened
¼ cup sugar
½ teaspoon grated lemon peel
½ cup milk
½ teaspoon vanilla
1½ cups all-purpose flour
1½ teaspoons baking powder
¼ teaspoon salt
2 stiff-beaten egg whites
1 10-ounce package frozen
    raspberries, thawed
1 10-ounce package frozen
    peach slices, thawed
¼ cup sugar
4 teaspoons cornstarch

In small mixing bowl cream butter or margarine, ¼ cup sugar, and the lemon peel. Combine milk and vanilla. Stir together flour, baking powder, and salt; beat into creamed mixture alternately with milk mixture. Fold in the egg whites. Lightly grease six 6-ounce custard cups or line cups with paper bake cups. Divide batter among cups.

Pour boiling water into wok to reach ½ inch below steamer rack. Place custard cups on rack. Cover wok and steam about 25 minutes or till knife inserted off-center comes out clean. Remove from custard cups.

Drain raspberries and peaches, reserving syrup. In small saucepan combine ¼ cup sugar and the cornstarch; stir in reserved syrup. Cook and stir till thickened and bubbly. Cook and stir 2 minutes more. Cool slightly; stir in fruit. Serve over steamed cakes. Makes 6 servings.

Spicy Poached Pears

¾ cup dry white wine
⅓ cup orange juice
¼ cup packed brown sugar
2½ inches stick cinnamon *or* 1
    teaspoon ground cinnamon
6 large pears, peeled, halved,
    and cored
Shredded orange peel
    (optional)
Vanilla *or* chocolate ice cream

In wok combine wine, orange juice, brown sugar, and cinnamon. Cook and stir over medium-low heat till sugar dissolves. Add pear halves; cover and cook 8 to 10 minutes or till pears are barely tender. Uncover; cook about 20 minutes more till pears are translucent. Remove stick cinnamon; cool slightly. Garnish with orange peel, if desired. Serve warm with ice cream. Makes 6 servings.

Brandy-Peach Sauce

2 pounds fresh peaches
    (6 medium)
⅓ cup sugar
¼ cup water
¼ cup lemon juice
¼ teaspoon ground nutmeg
¼ cup sliced almonds, toasted
¼ cup peach brandy *or* brandy
Vanilla ice cream

Peel peaches; slice, removing pits. In wok combine sugar, water, lemon juice, and nutmeg. Bring to boiling. Add peach slices; reduce heat. Cover and simmer about 10 minutes or till tender, stirring occasionally. Stir in almonds and peach brandy. Heat through. Serve warm over ice cream. Makes 6 to 8 servings.

Flaming Peaches: Prepare recipe as directed above, *except* reserve *half* of the brandy. Heat the reserved brandy in a small saucepan or large ladle till just warm. Ignite with a long match; pour over peach mixture. When flame dies, stir before spooning over ice cream.

Strawberries Flambé

2 10-ounce packages frozen
   sliced strawberries *or* whole
   raspberries, thawed
2 teaspoons cornstarch
2 tablespoons lemon juice
¼ cup slivered almonds, toasted
2 tablespoons orange liqueur
   Chocolate ice cream

Drain berries, reserving syrup. In wok stir reserved syrup into cornstarch; stir in lemon juice. Bring to boiling; cook and stir 2 minutes. Stir in berries and almonds; heat 1 minute longer. Heat liqueur in a small saucepan or large ladle till just warm; ignite with a long match and pour over berry mixture. When flame dies, stir and serve immediately over ice cream. Makes 6 to 8 servings.

Flaming Cranberries á la Mode

½ cup honey
1 teaspoon finely shredded
   orange peel
½ cup orange juice
¼ cup sugar
3 cups fresh cranberries*
¼ cup brandy (optional)
   Vanilla ice cream

In wok combine honey, orange peel, orange juice, and sugar; stir in cranberries. Boil gently about 5 minutes or till skins pop and mixture is slightly thickened. In small saucepan or large ladle, heat brandy over low heat till just warm. Ignite; pour over berry mixture. Stir after flame dies. Serve over ice cream. Makes 8 servings.

   *Recipe note: Frozen cranberries can substitute for fresh ones in this recipe.

Spicy Dried Fruit Compote *(pictured on pages 72 and 73)*

2 8-ounce packages mixed dried
   fruits
1 cup raisins
2½ cups orange juice
½ cup sugar
2 lemon slices
10 whole cloves
6 inches stick cinnamon

Cut up any large pieces of dried fruits. In wok place mixed dried fruits and raisins. Stir in orange juice and sugar. Bring to boiling. Stud lemon slices with cloves; add to wok. Add stick cinnamon. Reduce heat; cover and simmer about 20 minutes or till fruit is tender. Discard lemon slices and stick cinnamon. Cool slightly. Spoon into serving dishes; top with whipped cream, if desired. Makes 8 to 10 servings.

Flaming Desserts

Surprise and delight guests by flaming a dessert in your wok. It's easy enough for every day, but special enough for a party. Choose spirits that are at least 70 proof. Liquor that has been open for some time may be hard to flame, so test yours beforehand. To flambé, pour liquor into a small saucepan or large ladle, and heat over low heat or a candle till liquor is just warm. Use a long match to ignite spirits, then pour the flaming liquor into the wok.

DESSERTS

Bananas with Pine Nuts

3 firm medium bananas
2 tablespoons butter
3 tablespoons honey
¼ cup pine nuts *or* pecans, toasted*
¼ cup raisins
4 teaspoons orange liqueur (optional)

Peel and bias-slice bananas into ½-inch pieces. In wok melt butter over medium heat; stir in honey. Add bananas, turning to coat. Cook 1 minute or till bananas are hot and glazed; *do not overcook*. Remove from heat; stir in nuts and raisins. Spoon into 4 dessert dishes; top *each* with *1 teaspoon* liqueur. Serve at once. Makes 4 servings.

*Recipe note: To toast nuts, spread in shallow baking pan. Toast in 350° oven about 10 minutes; stir occasionally.

Banana Fritters

1 cup all-purpose flour
¼ cup sugar
2 teaspoons baking powder
1 teaspoon salt
¼ teaspoon ground nutmeg
1 beaten egg
½ cup milk
1 tablespoon cooking oil
1 teaspoon vanilla
    Cooking oil for deep-fat frying
3 bananas, cut into 1-inch pieces
    Hot fudge sauce, maple syrup, *or* powdered sugar

In bowl stir together flour, sugar, baking powder, salt, and nutmeg. Combine egg, milk, 1 tablespoon oil, and vanilla; stir into dry ingredients till smooth.

In wok heat 2 inches oil to 375°. Dip banana pieces into batter; fry a few at a time in hot oil for 2 to 3 minutes or till golden. Drain on paper toweling. Serve with hot fudge sauce or maple syrup, or sprinkle with powdered sugar. Makes 4 servings.

Pineapple Fritters: Substitute one 15½-ounce can *pineapple slices,* well drained and halved, for the bananas in recipe above.

Apple Fritters: Peel and core 3 large *apples;* cut into ½-inch slices. Substitute for bananas in recipe above.

Strawberry Fritters: Hull 18 large *strawberries;* substitute for bananas in recipe above.

Pigs' Ears

2 cups all-purpose flour
1 teaspoon baking powder
½ teaspoon salt
2 eggs
½ cup butter *or* margarine, melted and cooled
    Cooking oil for deep-fat frying
1½ cups cane syrup *or* 1 cup dark corn syrup *plus* ½ cup light molasses
¾ cup coarsely chopped pecans

Stir together flour, baking powder, and salt; set aside. In deep bowl beat eggs with fork; gradually beat in cooled butter. Stir into flour mixture till well mixed. Divide and shape dough into 24 balls. On lightly floured surface roll each ball into a paper-thin round about 6 inches in diameter. Cover to prevent drying.

In wok heat 2 inches oil to 365°. Place 1 dough round in hot oil; as soon as it rises to surface, pierce center with long-handled fork and rotate clockwise, pressing fork and dough against side of wok till shape is set. Fry 1 to 1½ minutes or till golden. Drain on paper toweling; keep warm while frying remaining rounds. In 2-quart saucepan bring cane syrup (or corn syrup and molasses) to boiling; cook over medium heat, stirring often, till thermometer registers 230°. Drizzle hot syrup over warm pastries; sprinkle with pecans. Serve warm or at room temperature. Makes 24.

Banana Fritters, Strawberry Fritters, Apple Fritters

DESSERTS

Sweet Fried Puffs

½ cup water
¼ cup butter *or* margarine
2 teaspoons sugar
Dash salt
½ cup all-purpose flour
2 eggs
Cooking oil for deep-fat frying
½ cup sugar
1 teaspoon ground cinnamon

In saucepan combine water, butter, 2 teaspoons sugar, and the salt. Bring to boiling, stirring till butter melts. Add flour all at once; cook and stir over low heat till mixture forms a ball that does not separate. Remove from heat; cool 10 minutes. Vigorously beat in eggs, one at a time, till mixture is smooth and shiny.

In wok heat 1½ inches oil to 375°. Drop dough by rounded teaspoonfuls into hot oil; fry a few at a time about 4 minutes or till golden brown, turning once. Drain on paper toweling. In a paper or plastic bag combine the ½ cup sugar and the cinnamon. Shake warm puffs in sugar mixture to coat. Makes about 20.

Sugar Plum Pudding

1 cup all-purpose flour
¾ cup sugar
½ teaspoon baking soda
½ teaspoon ground nutmeg
½ teaspoon ground cinnamon
¼ teaspoon salt
⅛ teaspoon ground cloves
2 beaten eggs
½ cup buttermilk
⅓ cup cooking oil
¼ cup chopped pitted prunes *or* raisins
½ cup chopped pecans *or* walnuts
Powdered sugar *or* Hard Sauce

In bowl stir together flour, sugar, soda, nutmeg, cinnamon, salt, and cloves. Stir together eggs, buttermilk, and oil; add to dry ingredients. Stir to mix well. Stir in fruit and nuts. Turn mixture into a greased and floured 8x4x2-inch loaf pan; cover with foil.

Pour boiling water into wok to reach ½ inch below steamer rack. Place loaf pan on rack; cover wok and steam 60 to 70 minutes or till cake tests done. Cool 10 minutes in pan; remove. Cool on a wire rack. Sprinkle with powdered sugar or serve with Hard Sauce. Makes 8 servings.

Hard Sauce: In small mixer bowl cream ½ cup softened *butter or margarine* and 2 cups sifted *powdered sugar* with electric mixer. Beat in 1 teaspoon *vanilla*. Spread mixture in a 7½x3½x2-inch loaf pan. Chill to harden; cut into squares to serve.

Apple-Bread Pudding

3 cups dry bread cubes (4 slices)
1 15-ounce jar chunk-style applesauce
⅓ cup raisins
2 beaten eggs
2 cups milk
½ cup sugar
1 teaspoon vanilla
⅛ teaspoon ground cinnamon
Dash salt
Dash ground nutmeg

In buttered 8x8x2-inch baking pan layer *half* of the bread cubes. Spread with applesauce; sprinkle with raisins and remaining bread cubes. Beat together eggs, milk, sugar, vanilla, cinnamon, salt, and nutmeg till well combined. Pour over bread mixture. Cover with foil.

Pour boiling water into wok to reach ½ inch below steamer rack. Place pan on rack; cover wok and steam about 45 minutes or till knife inserted off center comes out clean. Makes 6 servings.

Maple Gingerbread *(pictured on pages 72 and 73)*

2 cups all-purpose flour
1 teaspoon ground ginger
¾ teaspoon baking soda
¼ teaspoon ground cloves
2 tablespoons chopped candied
   ginger
¼ cup butter *or* margarine,
   softened
⅓ cup packed brown sugar
2 eggs
¾ cup maple-flavored syrup
2 tablespoons milk
⅓ cup maple-flavored syrup
½ teaspoon finely shredded
   lemon peel
2 tablespoons lemon juice

Combine flour, ground ginger, soda, cloves, and ¼ teaspoon *salt;* stir in chopped ginger to coat. In small mixer bowl beat butter for 30 seconds. Add sugar; beat till fluffy. Add eggs, one at a time, beating 1 minute after each. Combine ¾ cup syrup and milk. Add dry ingredients and syrup mixture alternately to beaten mixture, beating after each addition just till blended. Turn into a greased and floured 6½-cup ring mold. Cover loosely with foil, leaving hole in center uncovered to allow steam to circulate.

Pour boiling water into wok to reach ½ inch below steamer rack. Place mold on rack. Cover wok and steam for 35 to 40 minutes or till cake tests done. Cool in pan 10 minutes; invert onto serving plate. In saucepan combine ⅓ cup syrup, lemon peel, and juice; bring to boiling. Pour over warm cake. Garnish with lemon slices and leaves, if desired. Serve at once. Makes 8 servings.

Steamed Blueberry Pudding

1 cup whole wheat flour
1 cup all-purpose flour
½ cup sugar
2 teaspoons baking powder
1 teaspoon ground cinnamon
½ teaspoon salt
⅓ cup butter *or* margarine
1 beaten egg
1 cup milk
1 cup fresh *or* frozen
   blueberries
   Cream Cheese Topper

In bowl mix flours, sugar, baking powder, cinnamon, and salt. Cut in butter till mixture resembles fine crumbs. Stir together egg and milk; add to flour mixture. Stir till well mixed; fold in blueberries. Pour into a greased and floured 5½-cup mold; cover tightly with foil.

Pour boiling water into wok to reach ½ inch below steamer rack. Place mold on rack; cover wok and steam 2 hours or till pudding tests done with wooden pick. Remove to a wire rack; uncover. Cool 15 to 20 minutes. Unmold; serve with Cream Cheese Topper. Makes 6 to 8 servings.

Cream Cheese Topper: Beat one 3-ounce package softened *cream cheese,* ¼ cup softened *butter or margarine,* 1 teaspoon *vanilla,* and ¼ teaspoon finely shredded *lemon peel* till fluffy. Slowly beat in 1 cup sifted *powdered sugar.* Stir in 2 tablespoons *milk;* beat till smooth.

Toasted Coconut Custard *(pictured on the cover)*

3 eggs
1½ cups light cream *or* milk
¼ cup sugar
2 teaspoons vanilla
¼ cup flaked coconut, toasted

Beat eggs with rotary beater or fork; stir in cream or milk, sugar, and vanilla. Stir in coconut. Divide mixture among 4 buttered 6-ounce custard cups. Cover each loosely with foil. Pour boiling water into wok to reach ½ inch below steamer rack. Arrange custard cups on rack. Cover wok and steam about 10 minutes or till knife inserted in center of custard comes out clean. Uncover; garnish with more toasted coconut, if desired. Makes 4 servings.

SNACKS & APPETIZERS

From popcorn for everyday snacking to cocktail party meatballs and chicken wings, woks provide fun food. Or, mix and match bread or pastry wrappers with sweet or savory fillings to create your own snacks.

Fried Pastries with
Fruit and Nut Filling
(see recipes, page 89)

Tortilla Pies with
Chicken-Bacon Fill-
ing (see recipes,
pages 88 and 89)

Pictured below:
Steamed Buns (see
recipe, page 86)

SNACKS & APPETIZERS

Wok Popcorn

2 tablespoons cooking oil
⅓ cup unpopped popcorn
  Salt
  Butter *or* margarine, melted
    (optional)

Heat wok over medium-high heat; add oil. Add 2 or 3 kernels popcorn; cover. When corn pops, add remaining popcorn to wok. Cover and cook over medium-high heat till popping stops; you need not shake the wok. Sprinkle popcorn with salt, and drizzle with melted butter or margarine, if desired. Makes 5 to 8 cups.

Popcorn Italiano

6 cups popped corn
3 tablespoons butter *or*
    margarine
½ teaspoon dried oregano,
    crushed
⅛ teaspoon garlic powder
  Dash pepper
¼ cup grated Parmesan cheese

Prepare popcorn in wok as directed above; turn into a large bowl. In wok melt butter or margarine over medium-high heat. Add oregano, garlic powder, and pepper. Remove from heat; stir in Parmesan cheese. Pour over popcorn; toss to mix well. Serve at once. Makes 6 cups.

Toasted Snack Mix

¼ cup butter *or* margarine
2 teaspoons Worcestershire
    sauce
¼ teaspoon garlic powder
¼ teaspoon celery salt
¼ teaspoon bottled hot pepper
    sauce
2 cups unsalted peanuts *or*
    almonds
2 cups thin pretzel sticks
2 cups round oat cereal

In wok melt butter or margarine over medium heat; stir in Worcestershire sauce, garlic powder, celery salt, and hot pepper sauce. Add nuts; cook over medium heat about 4 minutes or till lightly browned, stirring constantly. Add pretzel sticks and cereal. Toss to coat well; continue to cook over medium heat, stirring constantly, about 1 minute or till slightly toasted. Cool before serving. Makes 6 cups.

Spicy Sugared Nuts

¾ cup sugar
¼ cup water
½ teaspoon ground cinnamon
¼ teaspoon ground allspice
⅛ teaspoon salt
1½ cups pecan *or* walnut halves

In wok combine sugar, water, cinnamon, allspice, and salt. Bring mixture to a full rolling boil. Boil gently for 4 minutes, stirring frequently. Remove from heat. Add pecans or walnuts; stir just till nuts are well coated. Turn mixture out onto waxed paper or foil; using 2 forks, quickly separate the nuts into bite-size clusters. Cool thoroughly before serving. Makes about ¾ pound.

Marinated Chicken Wings

12 **chicken wings (2 pounds total)**
¼ **cup soy sauce**
¼ **cup dry sherry**
1 **tablespoon sugar**
2 **cloves garlic, minced**
½ **teaspoon ground ginger**
⅓ **cup all-purpose flour**
  Cooking oil for deep-fat frying

Remove and discard wing tips; separate remaining joints. Place wing pieces in plastic bag set in deep bowl. Combine soy sauce, sherry, sugar, garlic, and ginger; pour over wings. Close bag; refrigerate several hours, turning occasionally. Drain, reserving marinade. Add water to marinade to make ⅔ cup; stir into flour. Beat smooth.

In wok heat 2 inches oil to 375°. Dip wings in flour mixture to coat; fry ⅓ at a time 5 minutes or till golden. Drain on paper toweling; keep warm. Makes 24.

Stuffed Beignets

1 **cup water**
½ **cup butter or margarine**
⅛ **teaspoon salt**
1 **cup all-purpose flour**
4 **eggs**
⅓ **cup grated Parmesan or Romano cheese, or finely shredded sharp cheddar cheese**
½ **teaspoon Worcestershire sauce**
1 **6- or 8-ounce can small whole mushrooms, drained**
  Cooking oil for deep-fat frying

In saucepan bring water, butter or margarine, and salt to boiling, stirring to melt butter. Add flour all at once; beat vigorously by hand till well blended. Cook and stir till mixture forms a ball that doesn't separate. Cool 5 minutes. Add eggs, one at a time, beating till smooth after each. Beat in cheese and Worcestershire sauce till blended. (Batter should be smooth, thick, and slightly sticky to the touch.) Drop *half* the batter by teaspoonfuls onto waxed paper. Place a whole mushroom atop each; top each with a teaspoonful of remaining batter to cover mushroom.

In wok heat 1½ inches oil to 375°. Fry beignets a few at a time for 5 to 6 minutes or till crisp and golden. Drain on paper toweling; serve warm. Makes about 40.

Fried Cheese with Tomato Sauce

1 **tablespoon butter or margarine**
1 **8-ounce can tomato sauce**
1 **2-ounce can mushrooms, drained and finely chopped**
½ **teaspoon dried oregano, crushed**
½ **teaspoon dried basil, crushed**
1 **cup fine dry bread crumbs**
1 **cup wheat germ**
¼ **teaspoon ground red pepper**
1 **pound cheese, well chilled***
4 **beaten eggs**
  Cooking oil for deep-fat frying

For sauce, in small saucepan melt butter or margarine; stir in tomato sauce, chopped mushrooms, oregano, and basil. Bring to boiling; reduce heat. Boil gently, uncovered, for 5 minutes, stirring occasionally. Cover and keep warm while frying cheese.

In small bowl combine bread crumbs, wheat germ, and red pepper. Cut cheese into 2x½x½-inch sticks or 1-inch cubes. Dip each piece of cheese into eggs, then into crumbs to coat well.

In wok heat 1½ inches oil to 375°. Fry a few cheese pieces at a time for ½ to 1 minute or till golden on all sides. Drain well on paper toweling; serve warm with tomato sauce. Makes 40 sticks or 20 cubes.

*Cheese suggestions: Swiss, Monterey Jack, Muenster, cheddar, fontina, Gouda, Edam, Havarti, Bel Paese, Brie, caraway cheese, or Camembert.

SNACKS & APPETIZERS

Cocktail Sausages

½ cup currant jelly
¼ cup dry red wine
½ teaspoon finely shredded
    lemon peel
2 tablespoons lemon juice
2 teaspoons prepared mustard
2 5-ounce packages small
    smoked sausage links*
1 tablespoon cold water
2 teaspoons cornstarch

In wok combine jelly, wine, lemon peel, lemon juice, and mustard. Bring to boiling; stir till jelly melts. Add sausages; cover and simmer 5 minutes. Stir water into cornstarch; stir into wok. Cook and stir till thickened and bubbly; cook and stir 2 minutes more. Serve warm with cocktail picks. Makes about 30.

*Recipe note: Other sausages work equally well in this recipe. Try two 5-ounce cans Vienna sausages, drained and halved; two 5-ounce packages cocktail wieners; or one 12-ounce package frankfurters, cut into 1-inch pieces.

Sweet-Sour Ham Balls

1 beaten egg
1 tablespoon milk
¼ cup finely crushed
    gingersnaps
¼ cup chopped green onion
1 clove garlic, minced
½ pound ground fully cooked
    ham
½ pound ground pork
2 tablespoons cooking oil
2 stalks celery, bias-sliced into
    1-inch pieces (1 cup)
1 15½-ounce can pineapple
    chunks
½ cup water
2 tablespoons vinegar
1 teaspoon instant chicken
    bouillon granules
¼ to ⅓ cup finely crushed
    gingersnaps

In bowl combine egg, milk, ¼ cup crushed gingersnaps, green onion, and garlic. Add ham and pork; mix well. Shape into small meatballs, using about 1 tablespoon mixture for each meatball.

Heat wok over high heat; add oil. Cook *half* the meatballs for 3 to 4 minutes or till lightly browned, shaking wok to rotate meatballs; remove from wok. Repeat with remaining meatballs; remove all from wok. Drain off all but 1 tablespoon drippings.

Add celery to wok; stir-fry 3 minutes. Stir in *undrained* pineapple, water, vinegar, and bouillon granules. Bring to boiling; stir in enough crushed gingersnaps to bring sauce to desired consistency. Return meatballs to wok; heat through. Serve meatballs warm with cocktail picks. Makes about 48 meatballs.

Keeping Food Hot

Your wok is an attractive serving dish for hot dips, meatballs, and other hot hors d'oeuvres. If yours is electric, simply set it on the table on a low heat setting to keep the food at serving temperature. Place conventional woks on a warming tray to keep food warm. If your wok has a flat bottom, set it directly on the warming tray. If not, set the wok in its ring stand (wide end up) on the tray. Or, use an electric hot plate on a low heat setting to keep food appetizingly warm.

Beer-Cheese Dip

1 cup beer
1 tablespoon all-purpose flour
8 ounces American cheese, cubed (2 cups)
1 8-ounce package cream cheese, cubed
1 teaspoon dry mustard
Dash garlic powder
1 3-ounce package smoked sliced beef, finely snipped
Vegetable dippers (such as carrot sticks, celery sticks, cucumber spears, radishes, green onions, cauliflower flowerets)

In wok heat beer over medium-high heat. Toss flour with American cheese; add to beer. Stir in cream cheese, mustard, and garlic powder. Cook and stir till mixture is smooth and slightly thickened. Stir in beef; heat through. Serve warm with assorted vegetable dippers. Makes about 3 cups.

Beer-Boiled Shrimp

1 12-ounce can beer
4 whole cloves
2 cloves garlic, minced
1 bay leaf
1 teaspoon salt
½ teaspoon dried dillweed
¼ teaspoon pepper
1 pound fresh or frozen shelled shrimp
Melted butter or cocktail sauce

In wok combine beer, cloves, garlic, bay leaf, salt, dillweed, and pepper. Bring to boiling over high heat; boil 5 minutes. Add shrimp; return to boiling. Cook 3 to 5 minutes or till shrimp turn pink. Drain; discard cloves and bay leaf. Serve shrimp hot with melted butter or cold with cocktail sauce. Makes 8 appetizer servings.

Crunchy Meatball Fondue

½ cup finely crushed shredded wheat biscuits
1 8-ounce container sour cream dip with French onion or sour cream dip with bacon and horseradish
¼ teaspoon garlic salt
Dash pepper
½ pound ground beef
Cooking oil for deep-fat frying
1 teaspoon salt

In bowl combine ¼ cup of the crushed wheat biscuits, ¼ cup of the dip, the garlic salt, and pepper. Add ground beef; mix well. Shape mixture into about 30 small meatballs; roll in the remaining crushed wheat biscuits to coat. Cover and refrigerate up to 24 hours.
In wok heat 1½ inches cooking oil to 350°. Add salt. Spear each meatball with fondue fork; fry in hot oil about 1½ minutes or till browned. Serve with remaining sour cream dip for dipping. Makes 30 meatballs.

WRAPPERS & FILLINGS

Create an impressive array of snacks and appetizers from the wrappers and fillings on the next 7 pages. Combine any filling with any wrapper to create your own favorites.

Steamed Buns *(pictured on pages 80 and 81)*

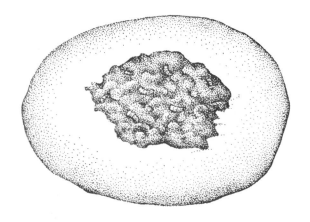

1¼ **to 1½ cups all-purpose flour**
  1 **package active dry yeast**
  ½ **cup milk**
  2 **tablespoons cooking oil**
  1 **tablespoon sugar**
  ¼ **teaspoon salt**
  1 **cup filling**

In mixer bowl combine ½ *cup* of the flour and the yeast. In saucepan heat together milk, oil, sugar, and salt just till warm (115° to 120°). Add to dry mixture in bowl. Beat at low speed of electric mixer for ½ minute, scraping sides of bowl constantly. Beat 3 minutes at high speed. Stir in as much of the remaining flour as you can mix in with a spoon. Turn out onto lightly floured surface. Knead in enough of the remaining flour to make a moderately stiff dough (6 to 8 minutes total). Place in lightly greased bowl; turn once to grease surface. Cover; let rise in a warm place till double (about 1 hour). Punch dough down; turn out onto lightly floured surface. Shape into 12 balls. Cover; let rest 5 minutes.

On lightly floured surface, roll each ball of dough to a 3-inch round. Place a heaping tablespoon of filling in center of each round. Bring edges of dough up around filling till edges just meet; pinch to seal in center, forming a small ball. Cover; let rise 10 minutes.

Pour boiling water into wok to reach ½ inch below steamer rack. Place buns, seam side down, on lightly greased steamer rack so sides don't touch; do not allow to rise. (If all buns won't fit on steamer rack, refrigerate some while others steam.) Place steamer rack over boiling water. Cover wok; steam buns 20 to 25 minutes or till done. Cool slightly before serving. Makes 12.

Recipe note: If you line the steamer rack with cabbage leaves before adding the buns, you won't have to grease the rack, and the buns won't stick. Be sure to leave some openings unobstructed so steam can circulate.

Cornmeal Tamales

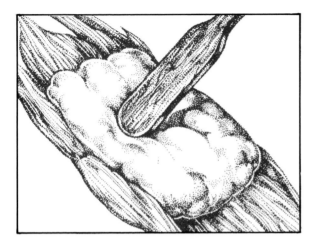
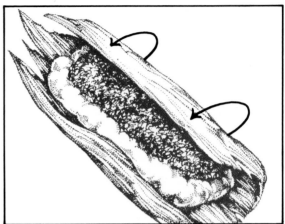

Cornhusks, parchment, *or* foil
2 cups water
¼ cup butter *or* margarine
1 teaspoon salt
1 cup cornmeal
1 cup water
1½ cups filling

Soak cornhusks in warm water several hours or overnight. Pat with paper toweling to remove excess moisture. (Or, cut parchment or foil into 8x6-inch rectangles.)

In wok bring the 2 cups water, the butter, and salt to boiling. combine cornmeal and the 1 cup water. Slowly add to the boiling mixture, stirring constantly. Cook and stir till mixture boils. Reduce heat; cover and cook over low heat about 15 minutes, stirring occasionally. Remove to another container; cool slightly.

Using about 2 tablespoons dough for each, spread to a 5x3-inch rectangle on each cornhusk or parchment or foil rectangle, placing one long edge of dough at one long edge of wrapper. Spread 1 tablespoon filling along center of dough, bringing out to ends, as shown above. Roll up, starting with long edge near dough. Tie ends with string or twist foil ends to seal.

Pour boiling water into wok to reach ½ inch below steamer rack. Arrange tamales on rack. Cover wok and steam 15 to 20 minutes or till heated through. Unwrap. Makes about 24.

Barbecue Ham Filling

3 tablespoons cooking oil
1½ cups finely chopped fully
   cooked ham
1 medium green pepper,
   chopped
1 clove garlic, minced
⅓ cup packed brown sugar
⅓ cup catsup
1½ teaspoons chili powder

Heat wok over high heat; add oil. Stir-fry ham, green pepper, and garlic for 5 minutes. Stir in brown sugar, catsup, and chili powder. Bring to boiling; boil for 2 to 3 minutes or till thickened. Cool slightly. Makes about 1½ cups.

WRAPPERS & FILLINGS

Tortilla Pies *(pictured on pages 80 and 81)*

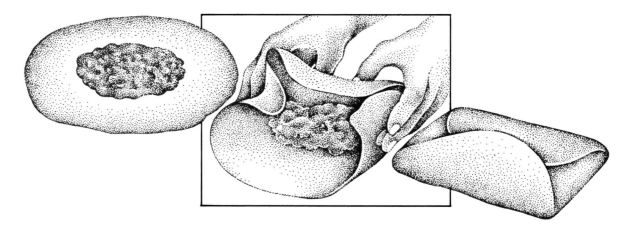

3 cups all-purpose flour
1½ teaspoons salt
1½ teaspoons baking powder
¼ cup shortening
¾ to 1 cup warm water
3 cups filling
    Cooking oil for deep-fat frying

In mixing bowl stir together flour, salt, and baking powder. Cut in shortening till mixture resembles cornmeal. Stir in ¾ cup water and mix till dough can be gathered into a ball; if needed, add more water, 1 tablespoon at a time. On lightly floured surface, knead dough 15 to 20 strokes or till smooth. Divide dough into 15 portions; cover and let dough rest for 15 minutes.

On floured surface, roll out one portion of dough to an 8-inch round. Cook on ungreased griddle or skillet about 1½ minutes on each side or till lightly browned. Repeat to make 15 tortillas.

Spoon about 3 tablespoons filling onto each tortilla. Fold sides in about 1 inch, then fold in bottom and top envelope fashion, as shown above, moistening edges with a little water.

In wok heat 2 inches of oil to 375°. Fry 2 pies at a time, seam side up, for 1 minute, using a spatula to hold tortillas under the oil. Remove spatula; fry about 1 minute longer or till golden. Drain well on paper toweling. Makes 15.

Sweet Cheese Filling

1½ cups cream-style cottage
    cheese, well drained, *or*
    ricotta cheese
2 tablespoons sugar
½ teaspoon vanilla
½ teaspoon finely shredded
    lemon peel
¼ cup finely chopped walnuts
2 tablespoons chopped raisins
    or dates

In small mixer bowl beat together the cottage cheese or ricotta cheese, sugar, vanilla, and lemon peel. Stir in nuts and raisins. Makes about 1½ cups.

Fried Pastries _(pictured on pages 80 and 81)_

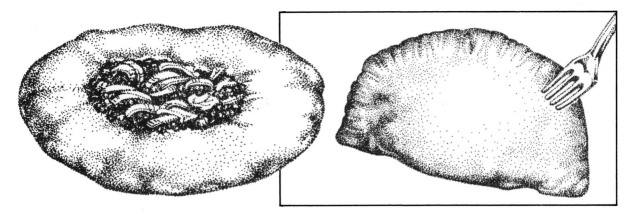

2	**cups all-purpose flour**
1	**teaspoon salt**
¼	**teaspoon coarsely ground pepper (optional)**
⅔	**cup shortening**
⅓ to ½	**cup cold water**
1½	**cups filling**
	Cooking oil for deep-fat frying

Stir together flour, salt, and pepper; cut in shortening till pieces are size of small peas. Sprinkle _1 tablespoon_ water over part of mixture. Gently toss with fork; push to side of bowl. Repeat till all is moistened. Divide dough in half. On floured surface roll each half to ⅛-inch thickness. Cut into 3-inch rounds. Place 1 heaping teaspoon filling in center of each; fold to make half-circle. Seal edges by pressing with tines of fork, as shown.

In wok heat 2 inches oil to 375°. Fry a few pastries at a time about 4 minutes or till golden, turning once. Drain on paper toweling. Makes about 32.

Fruit and Nut Filling _(pictured on pages 80 and 81)_

1½	**cups chopped walnuts _or_ pecans**
½	**cup strawberry preserves**
1	**teaspoon lemon juice**
¼	**teaspoon ground nutmeg**

Stir together walnuts or pecans, preserves, lemon juice, and nutmeg. Makes about 1½ cups.

Recipe note: Another time, substitute apricot or peach preserves for the strawberry preserves.

Chicken-Bacon Filling _(pictured on pages 80 and 81)_

3	**slices bacon, cut up**
¼	**cup pecan halves**
1	**cup chopped cooked chicken _or_ turkey**
⅓	**cup chopped celery**
½	**of an 8-ounce carton sour cream dip with onion**
⅛	**teaspoon salt**

In wok cook bacon over medium-high heat till nearly done. Drain off fat. Add pecans to wok; continue cooking bacon and pecans till bacon is crisp and pecans are toasted. Drain on paper toweling; cool slightly. Chop bacon and pecans. In bowl combine chicken, celery, bacon, and pecans. Add sour cream dip and salt; mix well. Makes about 1½ cups.

Fried Wontons

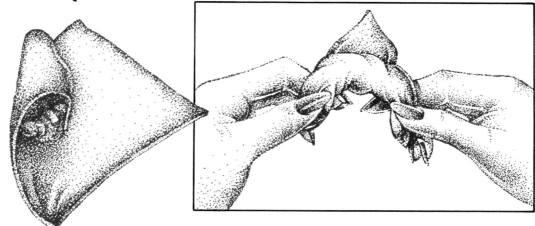

40 wonton skins*
1½ cups filling
Cooking oil for deep-fat frying

Separate wonton skins. Position a wonton skin with one point toward you. Spoon about 2 teaspoons filling just off center of skin. Fold bottom point of wonton skin over the filling; tuck point under filling, as shown above. Roll once to cover filling, leaving about 1 inch unrolled at top of skin. Moisten right corner of skin with water. Grasp the right and left corners of skin as shown; bring these corners toward you below the filling. Overlap left corner over right corner; press wonton skin securely to seal. Repeat with remaining wonton skins and filling.

In wok heat 1½ inches oil to 365°. Fry wontons, a few at a time, for 2 to 3 minutes or till golden. Drain on paper toweling; serve warm. Makes 40.

*Recipe note: Buy wonton·skins in the produce section of a large supermarket or Oriental specialty shop. If wonton skins are unavailable, purchase egg roll skins instead. Quarter each egg roll skin to make 4 wrappers the same size as wonton skins.

Savory Cheese Filling

1 beaten egg
1 cup ricotta cheese *or* cream-style cottage cheese, drained
½ cup grated Parmesan cheese
⅓ cup snipped parsley
½ teaspoon dried basil, crushed
¼ teaspoon pepper
Dash ground nutmeg

In bowl combine egg, ricotta or cottage cheese, Parmesan cheese, snipped parsley, basil, pepper, and nutmeg. Makes about 1½ cups.

Egg Rolls

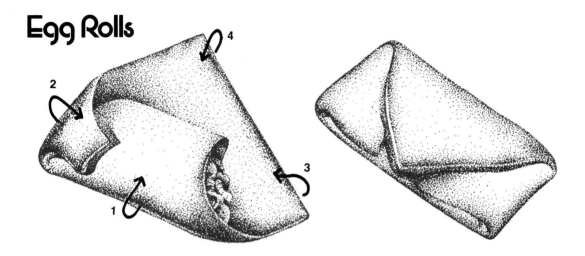

6 egg roll skins
1½ cups filling
Cooking oil for deep-fat frying

Separate egg roll skins. Position an egg roll skin with one point toward you. Spoon ¼ cup filling diagonally across and just below center of skin. Fold bottom point of skin over filling; tuck point under filling as shown above. Fold side corners over center, forming an envelope shape. Roll up egg roll toward remaining corner; moisten point with a little water and press firmly to seal. Repeat with remaining skins and filling.

In wok heat 2 inches oil to 365°. Fry 1 or 2 egg rolls at a time for 2 to 3 minutes or till golden brown. Drain on paper toweling; serve warm. Makes 6.

Recipe note: Traditionally, egg rolls and wontons are served with a sauce for dipping. Depending on the filling you choose, dip yours in prepared mustard, prepared horseradish, barbecue sauce, or an Oriental sweet-sour sauce. With a sweet filling, choose sour cream or whipped cream, or sprinkle the snack with powdered sugar.

Oriental Shrimp and Pork Filling

2 tablespoons soy sauce
1 tablespoon cornstarch
2 tablespoons cold water
1 teaspoon molasses
1 tablespoon cooking oil
1 clove garlic, minced
1 cup finely chopped cooked pork *or* beef
1 cup finely chopped cabbage
½ cup shredded carrot
1 4½-ounce can shrimp, rinsed, drained, and chopped

Blend soy sauce into the cornstarch; stir in water and molasses. Set aside.

Heat wok over high heat; add oil. Stir-fry garlic for 30 seconds. Add pork or beef, cabbage, and carrot; stir-fry 3 minutes. Stir in shrimp. Stir soy sauce mixture; stir into wok. Cook and stir 1 minute. Cool slightly before using. Makes about 2 cups.

FILLINGS

Dill-Tuna Filling

1 6½-ounce can tuna
¼ cup finely chopped dill pickle
¼ cup chopped toasted almonds
    or peanuts
2 tablespoons mayonnaise *or*
    salad dressing
2 tablespoons snipped parsley

Drain and flake the tuna. In a bowl stir together tuna, pickle, almonds or peanuts, mayonnaise or salad dressing, and snipped parsley. Makes about 1½ cups.

Apple-Pork Filling

1 tablespoon butter
¼ cup chopped green pepper
¼ cup chopped onion
1 cup chopped cooked pork
⅔ cup chopped peeled apple
2 tablespoons Dijon-style
    mustard
¾ teaspoon ground ginger
¼ teaspoon salt

In wok melt butter over medium-high heat. Add green pepper and onion; stir-fry for 3 minutes. Add pork; stir-fry 1½ minutes longer. Remove from heat; stir in apple, mustard, ginger, and salt. Makes about 1½ cups.

Beef and Cabbage Filling

½ pound ground beef
¼ cup chopped onion
½ teaspoon garlic salt
    Dash bottled hot pepper sauce
1½ cups shredded cabbage
3 tablespoons cold water
2 teaspoons all-purpose flour

In wok cook beef, onion, garlic salt, and pepper sauce over medium-high heat till meat is brown and onion is tender, breaking meat into small pieces. Drain off fat. Place cabbage over meat; add *1 tablespoon* water. Cover; cook over low heat 10 minutes or till cabbage is done. Stir remaining 2 tablespoons water into the flour; stir into wok. Cook and stir till thickened and bubbly; cook and stir 1 minute more. Cool slightly. Makes 1½ cups.

Franks-and-Sauerkraut Filling

½ pound frankfurters *or* fully
    cooked Polish sausage
1 8-ounce can sauerkraut
1 tablespoon butter
¼ cup chopped onion
⅓ cup beer
1 tablespoon prepared mustard

Chop frankfurters or Polish sausage. Drain and chop sauerkraut; set aside. In wok melt butter over medium-high heat. Add onion; stir-fry for 3 minutes or till onion is tender. Add meat; stir-fry 3 minutes longer or till meat is lightly browned. Stir in sauerkraut, beer, and mustard. Stir-fry over medium-high heat till all liquid evaporates. Cool slightly. Makes about 1¾ cups.

INDEX

INDEX